Ruminations

ON
COLLEGE
LIFE

by Aaron Karo

A FIRESIDE BOOK
Published by Simon & Schuster
New York • London • Toronto • Sydney • Singapore

FIRESIDE
Rockefeller Center
1230 Avenue of the Americas
New York, NY 10020

FIRESIDE and colophon are registered trademarks
of Simon & Schuster, Inc.

Portions of this book originally appeared in the ezine
Ruminations on College Life.

For information regarding special discounts for bulk purchases,
please contact Simon & Schuster Special Sales at
1-800-456-6798 or business@simonandschuster.com

DESIGNED BY ADAM W. COHEN

Manufactured in the Unites States of America

10   9   8   7   6   5   4

Library of Congress Cataloging-in-Publication Data
Karo, Aaron.
    Ruminations on college life / by Aaron Karo.
        p.   cm.
"A Fireside Book."
1. College students—Humor. I. Title.
PN6231.C6 K34 2002
378.1'98'0207—dc21   2002066904
ISBN 0-7432-3293-3

Dedicated to
the Brothers of Zeta Beta Tau,
whose model behavior was an inspiration

Acknowledgments

I WOULD LIKE to thank the two most important people in the world to me, my amazing parents, Helene and Al Karo. Throughout the past four years, they supported me with both words of encouragement and monthly checks. Though they blindly financed my excessive drinking habits, they never discouraged me from writing about them. I know I can always count on their love and support.

My sister, Caryn, who is now living through her own *Ruminations* at Dartmouth, has always been my best friend. Throughout my life she has been there for me, usually with kind words like, "Aaron, you're not funny" or "I'm telling Mom you threw up." Caryn has always kept me in line, and for that I love her more than anything.

I would also like to thank all my friends, both from the University of Pennsylvania and from back home in Plainview, New York. In the end, this book is really about them. It's filled with their hilarious quotes and drunken stories. Of course, when I told them about the book, their first response was invariably either "So, do I get a cut?" or "Yo, you're not gonna put that story about me and that chick in there are you?" Some things never change.

I also owe a debt of gratitude to my manager, A. B. Fischer, and my editor, Allyson Edelhertz, both of whom played major roles in transforming the drunken ramblings of a sleepless college student into, well, the drunken ramblings of a sleepless college student with a table of contents. They were the first to see the real potential of *Ruminations* and for that I am eternally grateful.

Finally, this book is for college students everywhere. We live stress-filled lives. Between classes and exams and drinking and friends and sleep and parents, we barely have enough time to pick up a book. However, I hope college kids around the world will read this and take solace. Because no matter how brutal the all-nighter or painful the hangover, you can always use a good laugh.

Note to the Reader

Several passages in this book contain stories involving excessive and underage drinking. I am in no way condoning such behavior. I mean, it's fun and may help you get laid, but it's dangerous nonetheless. For your own safety, if you drink, please do so somewhat responsibly. *Thank you.*

-Karo

contents

Welcome to College Life

When I first arrived on campus at the University of Pennsylvania, I quickly gained the "Freshman 15"—the ability to drink fifteen beers in one sitting. My first couple of weeks as a freshman were typical. I wandered around completely clueless and partied so hard that it made even my wildest high school nights seem tame in comparison. I rarely stumbled back to my tiny dorm room before 4 A.M.

On Sunday nights I would try to take a break from the drunken mayhem and rest up for the coming week. However, since my body was so messed up from the weekend's festivities, I could never fall asleep. As I tossed and turned for hours, all these funny thoughts and observations about college life kept bouncing around in my head. One Sunday night I finally decided to write them down, and the next day I emailed them to twenty of my friends from high school. *Ruminations on College Life* was born.

Each month throughout my freshman year I continued to email out an issue of *Ruminations*. The emails consisted of all my funny stories and anecdotes about college life that I thought up on sleepless Sunday nights. Soon my friends began forwarding it to their friends, who then emailed me to be added to my mailing list.

As I kept writing during my sophomore year, my mailing list kept growing and growing, and I created AaronKaro.com to hold all the old issues. By my junior year, *Ruminations on College Life* had become an international phenomenon as thousands upon thousands of pre-froshes, college kids, and alumni joined my list. My issues were used to teach English to students in Finland and Austria and were the subject of term papers and class projects from Syracuse to UCLA.

By the time of my graduation from Penn in May 2001, I had over 11,000 subscribers around the world. The drunken ramblings of a sleepless college freshman had evolved into something I could never have imagined. After graduation I tried to get all my *Ruminations* published, the right people saw them, and the result is in your hands right now.

If you're reading this in the bookstore, take a look around. There are tons of books about college. Some will tell you what classes to take and others will tell you how to deal with an unruly roommate. But none will tell you what really goes down in the tiny dorm rooms and frat-house basements of colleges across the nation and around the world. This one will.

I hope you will read my book and laugh out loud. Because whether you're going to college soon, currently surviving it, or already a grizzled alum, the college experience is universal. It is also absurd and ridiculous. So get comfortable on your extra-long twin, crack open a case of cheap beer, and read on. And whatever campus you call home, always remember, college is a joke!

CHAPTER ONE

Freshman Year

Your freshman year of college is supposed to be a new beginning. You emerge from the summer following your graduation from high school pretty much hating your hometown and everyone in it. You look forward to college as a chance to start fresh, to make new friends and begin a new phase in your life. Then you get to college and immediately start hanging out with everyone who goes there from your high school, and you're constantly instant-messaging and emailing your friends from home. That's because freshman year isn't a whole new phase of your life; it's really just another place to participate in underage drinking and trying to get laid.

As a freshman, you're the lowest of the low. You don't know anybody, you can't find anything, and no one seems to want to explain anything to you. But everyone knows what it's like to be a freshman, so you have to use it to your advantage: "Excuse me, young man, why are you twenty minutes late for class?" Your response: "I'm sorry, I'm a freshman and I got lost." "Yo, dude, you just threw up all over my girlfriend!" Your response: "I'm sorry, I'm a freshman and I'm wasted." And they'll understand.

In the end, being a college freshman is like being a fetus. You're helpless, you still rely on your mom for pretty much everything, and you have no clue what the hell is going on. By the end of the year, you're wasted off your rocker, still completely clueless, and passed out on your dorm-room floor in the fetal position.

THE FIRST WEEK of college feels kind of like camp. You've got enough clothes to last you a few weeks, you're sleeping in a little bed, and you write letters to your parents and friends. After two months I was like, "OK, this has been fun, but the summer is over now, time to go home." The RA was in the hallway stopping dazed kids from leaving. They were all packed up saying, "Wait, you mean this isn't camp? But it feels just like camp! What? Four more years?"

WHEN I FIRST got to college, I was still kind of in that high school "gotta get involved" mode. You know, like when you used to join clubs just so you could put it on your college application. Anyway, for some reason I decided to run for freshman class president. Of course, I got trounced by some kid who was also still really into "getting involved," even more than me. (I think he needed it for his grad school application or something.) Even though I lost, I think I still had the best posters. They read VOTE KARO FOR PRESIDENT. PLEASE, I ALREADY TOLD MY MOM I WON! I thought that alone should have won me the election.

I WAS PRETTY prepared for college life right from the start because I had visited as a pre-frosh many times. There's nothing better than being a pre-frosh. You're so clueless but you have all of college still ahead of you. I'll never forget my first visit to campus. I got absolutely wasted and ended up on the floor of the dorm bathroom. This cute college girl comes in and asks me if I'm OK. I could barely respond. She said, "So you're a pre-frosh?" I nodded. She said, "OK, let me help you out," and proceeded to stick her fingers down my throat until

I threw up, which made me feel much better. I never found out who that mysterious girl was, but I think of her every time I vomit.

HOW HOT WERE the first few days of school? I had like fifteen fans going at once in my room and one mini one that I kept directly in my face all day. That's basically who my good friends are now—the ones who had the best fans, because I was always in their rooms. This one kid had an industrial-size fan and a grilled-cheese maker. He's my best friend now.

IN EVERY GRADUATING class from high school, there are always like five couples that decide to stay together when they go away to college. This always baffles me. Of all the couples from your school that did this, how many are still together? Zero! That's because it never works! Who are you kidding? Instead of talking to your boyfriend or girlfriend who is a thousand miles away on the phone ("Oh, I can't wait to see you over Thanksgiving break"), get a clue and start randomly hooking up like the rest of us.

A COUPLE OF weeks into my freshman year, when my

mom asked me if I knew my way around, I said yes. But what I really meant was, I can only find the one room I have class in, in each of only four buildings, the frat houses, the places that sell beer, anything open twenty-four hours, my room, twelve other kids' rooms, and the cheese steak place.

ARE YOU GOOD with names? I forget them as soon as I hear them. Might as well not tell me at all! I have no idea what anyone's names are except my own, the kids I went to high school with, and that one hot girl who I have never spoken to but stalk from afar.

I HAVE NO idea how to do laundry. No, no, not like I have some idea but just don't know how much fabric softener to use, I mean I have *no idea* how to do laundry. I just had this vision that there would be some cute chick in the laundry room every time I went there who would show me how to do it. Dreams die hard, but I have no underwear.

CAMPUS IS REALLY a communist society. I own nothing, it all belongs to the university. I have no money—it's all my parents'. My meals are served in little square portions at one brick building only during certain hours of the day! Is this college or the Soviet Union?

I LOVE THE concept of the dining hall. Because before you get to campus for the first time and you're deciding which meal plan to sign up for, older kids will always say the same thing: "The food is terrible but it's more of a social thing for freshmen." So we know going in that the food sucks! It's like we're saying, "Hey, Mom, I'm going away to college, but I don't really know anyone. So could you throw me a few thousand dollars? It's for peanut butter and jelly sandwiches and some friends."

FRESHMEN ARE ALWAYS saying, "I go to bed so late," "I don't sleep enough," "I have to catch up on my sleep." I get too much sleep. I'm sleeping all the time. I have to set my alarm just to wake up at 4 P.M. Catch up on sleep? I think I have to catch up on my *awake* because I have no clue what the hell goes on during the day!

DOES YOUR MOM still ask you about that kid you met the first day of school? You know, you meet this kind of dorky kid the first day and for some reason he'd already been there a week and knows everything, so he helps you move in. Every single time I speak to my mom now, she asks me about him. Like I know. I haven't even seen the kid since!

SO I'M OBSESSED with this gorgeous junior girl who of course won't give me the time of day. But I really don't understand why. I don't think she understands that, she being a gorgeous junior girl and me being a lowly freshman guy, the first eleven times we hooked up, she wouldn't even have to move. I swear I would do all the work—she could just lie on her back the whole time. Why wouldn't she want that? I don't understand!

MY FRIEND DAN, like me, has no idea how to do laundry. One day he's out of underwear, the girl down the hall won't do it for him anymore, and he's desperate. So he decides to give it a try. He goes down to the laundry room in the basement of the dorm and tries to figure it out. He puts his clothes in the machine, puts the detergent in, puts some quarters in, but the thing is not working. He tries everything, but it's just not happening. Completely bewildered, he sees a little red help button right next to the machine and presses it. Unfortunately, it was the emergency alarm. Sirens in the dorm start blaring, red lights are flashing everywhere, cops are on the scene in minutes, and my friend has to sneak back to his room amid all this chaos wearing only a towel. He never did his own laundry again.

WHEN WINTER COMES around, bringing increasingly cold weather and increasingly packed frat parties, freshmen become faced with the paradox of clothing. If you dress warmly for the walk to the party, you'll sweat to death inside the frat. But if you dress lighter, you'll freeze to death before you even make it in. So really the question is, before you die, wouldn't you rather have a couple of beers first?

AS MY FRESHMAN year of college drew to a close, I realized what a wild ride it had been. I have never consumed so many toxic substances, expelled so many body fluids, or done as much work as I did that year. I guess freshman year is kind of like an economics problem. You want to maximize toxic substances consumed, minimize body fluids expelled, and do a decent amount of work. Of course, that's all theory. In reality, I ended up doing twelve kegstands, puking my brains out, and sleeping through my econ quiz. I love college.

CHAPTER TWO

Life in the

Dorm

Have you ever noticed that in every TV show and movie made about college the dorm rooms are huge? Kids are throwing parties in there, they have couches, it's ridiculous. Let's set this straight once and for all: College kids live in what amounts to a glorified closet. We have to put our beds on cinderblocks just to have room for our clothes. Prisoners don't even have to do that! I literally had to Velcro my TV remote control to the wall because there was no place to put it.

Still, you know what the great thing about college dorms is? If you're lucky enough to have your own bathroom (or for guys, a sink will do), it's the only time in your life when you will have every necessary amenity in one room. You can have a bed, TV, toilet, refrigerator, and desk all within five feet of each other. I'm so lazy that I went out and bought a nice desk chair on wheels. By the end of the semester I didn't even get up anymore, I just swiveled and rolled.

No matter how small your dorm room is, though, it is where you will have some of your best college moments. It's where you will pre-game with your best friends. It's where you will boot when you've had one tequila shot too many. It's where you will fight with your roommate about his terrible taste in music. And it is where you will hook up with the girl down the hall and then try to avoid seeing her for the rest of the semester. And by the time you move out of the dorm, you'll realize, for a tiny room, you really got a lot of use out of it.

WHOEVER INVENTED YAFFA Blox must have made a fortune off college kids. Yaffa Blox are of course those plastic, removable shelves that every college kid has in their dorm room. Before I left for college I think my mom became obsessed with those things. She'd pace back and forth while I was packing, muttering, "Do you have enough Yaffa Blox? I think you may need more. OK, I'm going to the store to get you a few more sets. More Yaffa!" I had every make and model of Yaffa Blox in my tiny little dorm but no place to put them and nothing to put in them, so I just put the small ones in the drawers of the big ones and put them all under my bed.

AN ESSENTIAL PART of any dorm experience is the resident advisor, or RA. I don't want to hear any excuses or explanations—if you're an RA, you're a dork, plain and simple. Why? Well, let's figure this out. You're a senior. You still live in the freshman dorm. Your sole purpose in life is to get kids in trouble if they drink in their rooms. What a pathetic existence. When you meet your RA the first day of college at your floor meeting, he'll probably feed you some line like, "I don't care what you do as long as I don't see it." Well that's just swell, buddy, but you know what would be great? If you got the hell out of the dorm and left us alone. That way you wouldn't see anything!

AN IMPORTANT RITUAL in the life of anyone about to go to college for the first time is the trip with your mom to Bed, Bath & Beyond or Linens 'n Things to get all the supplies for your dorm room. It's a daunting task because you never know how much stuff you will actually need. You go in there thinking you'll need like a soap dish and a fan, and you come out with two shopping carts full of dust ruffles, egg crates, Yaffa Blox, and grilled-cheese makers, most of which you've never even heard of before and probably won't ever use.

WHY IS IT that no matter how much you pray when you first move into the dorm that a hot chick who only wants to hook up with you will move in next door, it always turns out to be a fat dude who smells?

YOU HAVE TO love the communal bathrooms in the dorm. When you have to take a dump, you go through that little ritual. You know what I'm talking about—first wipe down the seat, then put a strip of toilet paper on each side, and, depending on the size of the dump, maybe one on the back of the seat too. Like that little piece of single-ply generic-brand toilet paper does anything at all!

SPEAKING OF DORM bathrooms, all my friends who share a bathroom with just one roommate always brag about how great it is. Personally, I would rather share a toilet with ten other guys than just one. It's all about the uncertainty principle. When there's something disgusting on the toilet seat in a communal bathroom, you're never sure who did it. But if you only share the toilet with one other person, you know exactly who the dirty little sucker is—your roommate!

CONTINUING ON THE bathroom theme here for a moment, my dorm bathroom water has only two temperatures—off and thermonuclear hot. The shower's only use is to provide boiling water to make coffee. Even the toilet water is hot. When you flush, so much steam shoots out it's like Old Faithful!

THE MOST DIFFICULT part of taking a shower in the communal bathroom of a dorm is the take-your-towel-off-before-you-get-in-the-shower-but-don't-let-anyone-see-you-naked maneuver. It's really difficult! If you aren't quick enough, your towel will get soaked in the shower, and the dude using the sink right next to you will see all you have to offer. Plus, you have to get the towel to hang correctly on the hook while making sure not to let it touch the pool of urine right below. It's like an obstacle course!

AND DOESN'T IT suck when you get in the shower and realize that you only have a molecule of soap left? Of course, instead of getting out of the shower and getting more soap, I try to splice my molecule of soap so that it's enough to wash my body. I think that's how the first atom was spliced. Some scientist was in the shower and he ran out of soap. Of course, it doesn't work for me, so I end up washing my body with Pert Plus. And then I forget to buy more soap for tomorrow.

LET'S CONTINUE ON the shower situation. I don't know about your shower, but whoever designed my bathroom's shower curtain made it as aerodynamic as possible, so that the slightest gust of air blows it open. If someone slams the door hard enough while you're taking a shower, the curtain blows completely off! And of course it always happens when you're washing your face, so that your eyes are closed and you don't notice the curtain is gone for like two minutes.

HALFWAY THROUGH MY freshman year, we got a steam room in my hallway. Yeah, remember how I said that our bathroom water has only two temperatures, off and thermonuclear hot? Well, now the shower is broken. It's been running continuously for seven days! It's so hot it turned the place into a steam room. We all go in there and sit around in towels talking about the stock market. It's great.

I HAVE ONE of those tote baskets that I use to carry my soap (when I remember to buy some) and shampoo into the shower. It's gotten pretty disgusting, though. It's got all kinds of hair and soap scum on it. What I don't understand is how the thing got so dirty in the first place. It takes a shower every day! Of all my personal belongings, this basket bathes the most, yet it's so gross! I just don't get it.

HOW'S THE ELECTRICITY situation in your dorm room? My room breaks every fire-hazard law in the state of Pennsylvania. I have a surge protector plugged into a surge protector connected by three extension cords. And behind my desk, oh man, that's where stray wires go to die. If I ever spill a glass of water back there, the whole damn place will blow up.

DRY-ERASE BOARDS. Now there's a great invention. My pen was stolen the first night so now the thing is useless. And stupid me, I put it over the peephole by accident. Now I can't get the damn double-sided tape off and I'm stuck with an obsolete piece of glorified cardboard on my door and I can't see out. Who the hell stole my pen anyway? Is there some underground black market for pens whose mark can be erased so easily? I guess it's just one of those college mysteries.

IS YOUR HALLWAY like the Loud Music Awards? It seems that everybody is trying to blast their music as loud as possible. This one jerk went away for the weekend and left his stereo on full blast with that "Who Let the Dogs Out?" song on repeat. He's dead now.

DO YOU HAVE that one poster in your room that has fallen down every single day so far? And it's right over your bed so it falls on you in the middle of the night and scares the hell out of you? The funny thing is that you're always too lazy to put any extra tape on it to make it stick, so you put it back up knowing full well that it's going to fall down again in about twelve hours.

BEFORE I LEFT for winter break, my RA kept reminding me, "Clean out your fridge, don't forget to clean out your fridge!" And I'm thinking, Why would I clean it out now when I'm only going home for two weeks? I've been here for four months and I haven't cleaned it out once!

MOST COLLEGE DORMS have these extra-long twin-size beds. The name is kind of misleading. Extra-long? You're thinking, Wow, this thing's gonna be huge! Of course, you get to your room and you can't believe how tiny it is. You're like, "Where's the rest of it?" The real question is, how are you supposed to hook up on one of those things? You roll over once and you're on the floor. There's barely enough room for one person, let alone two! Of course, when I moved out of the dorm and got a big mattress, what did I do? I only slept on one edge of it.

SPEAKING OF BEDS, why do girls have so many pillows? Is this normal? Did you have that many pillows at home, or are you just showing off how many damn Polo Sport pillowcases you have?

WHY IS IT that when the fire alarm goes off in the dorm, everyone's first reaction is always, "There's no way there's a fire, it must be a false alarm"? That seems a little counterproductive to me.

WHY ON EARTH do grilled-cheese makers and George Foreman grills have no ON/OFF switch? Have you ever used one of these things? You have to yank it out of the wall to turn it off. Of all the appliances in the world, the ones most likely to be found in disgusting, beer-soaked dorm rooms and plugged into four interlocking surge protectors should definitely have an OFF switch.

THE SAVING OF empty beer and liquor bottles is a strange college phenomenon. I bet most of you college students reading this right now have some empties on a shelf in your room. Everyone knows how much college kids like to drink, do we really need to display it? It's a good thing, though, that this trend stops after college. Wouldn't it be weird if your parents had empty wine bottles up on their bedroom wall?

YOU GUYS HAVE that cup. I know you do. You know, that one all-purpose cup that you use for everything from cereal to orange juice to shots of Johnnie Walker Black Label and never clean? At the end of the week that thing is sticky as hell. And there's always that poor spoon that gets stuck in the cup forever.

EVER NOTICE THAT the only alarm clock that you can work is your own? Have you ever been woken up by a roommate's alarm clock at six in the morning? You stumble over to his nightstand and try to shut it off, but you try every single button and it won't stop beeping, so you end up having to yank it out of the wall like a George Foreman grill.

IS IT SOME kind of college entrance requirement that you have to love Dave Matthews? Because it seems like no dorm room is complete without it playing constantly in the background. And I love it when people say, "Oh, I love Dave!" Like they know him personally or something.

INEVITABLY, IF YOU drink enough, you'll have to puke. When you have to throw up, nothing will stop you from getting to the dorm bathroom. I'll be in my room and start getting that feeling in my throat, so I knock my chair down, bust open the door, sprint down the hallway and knock some chick down the stairs. That bathroom's locked, so I run up the stairs, barge into the women's bathroom, break down the stall door, and then what do I do? I throw up on the toilet paper dispenser, completely missing the toilet.

WHEN I MOVED into my dorm, I got this awesome new phone with speakerphone and all these great features. But have you ever noticed that you've never actually *used* speakerphone? That's because every time you try to use it, the person on the other end is like, "Take me off speakerphone, I can't hear you!"

THEY MUST GIVE college kids the phone numbers of people who didn't pay their bills and had their service shut off a week earlier, because I get more wrong numbers than right ones. But I just don't get why people who have the wrong number continually leave messages on my answering machine. The message clearly states, "Hey, this is Karo, I'm not here right now . . ." Yet every week I get at least one message like, "Hi, this message is for Leroy, your car is ready to be picked up . . ."

WHEN I MOVED out of the dorm, I had to change the addresses of my magazine subscriptions. So I started getting *Maxim* at my new address, no problem. Then one month the magazines just stopped coming. A few weeks later I get a little postcard in my mailbox from the magazine saying that I have an invalid address and they can no longer send me issues. Well, how the hell did you mail me this postcard then?

NOW THAT MOST of my friends have moved out of the dorms and into much bigger rooms in fraternity houses and apartments, I have noticed an evolution in the way they set up their rooms. Freshman year all you wanted to do was figure out how to fit that damn minifridge into your tiny room. Now you have to maximize the amount of seating while leaving enough elbow room for everyone sitting to chug a beer at once and minimize the amount of steps it takes to get a girl from your door to your bed.

WHY IS IT such a big deal to find out who lives in your old dorm room? You're always like, "Oh, I hope they're cool" or "Maybe a hot chick lives there now." How is that really going to help? What are you going to say? "Hey, baby, so I hear you live in room 336. You know that stain on the carpet? That was me." Oh yeah, she'll definitely go for that.

CHAPTER THREE

Life on

Campus

Much of college life revolves around the campus. For instance, you can live either off-campus or on-campus, there's no in between. I always found it interesting to try to figure out the exact point where campus went from "off" to "on." I think it comes down to learning. If you're learning something, in a classroom or a library, you're on-campus. No learning takes place off-campus. There are frat houses, bars, and apartments. Campus is where we go to get smart. Off-campus is where we go to get drunk and stupid.

I love how college brochures depict campus. There are students lying on the green reading books and studying. A couple of kids are engaged in a friendly Frisbee toss. Maybe there are even some fraternity members pitching in by painting a fence in front of the library. In reality, the kids on the grass are lying there because they're so hungover they can't stand up and are trying to copy the homework they didn't do in time for their next class. The frat boys are painting the fence, and doing a half-assed job at best, because they're trying to get their house off probation for throwing a party so loud that cops came from three neighboring states. And the Frisbee players? The brochure photographer probably just paid them off.

You see, college kids don't spend as much time actually *on* campus as they do passing *through* campus. As in walking to a frat party, running to a class you overslept, or stumbling home from the bar. And, in general, making the brochure photographer's job as hard as possible.

WHAT IS WITH these credit card companies who hire people to stand on the green and try to get your credit information in exchange for a free T-shirt? I feel like a rock star walking through campus. All these people I've never met are mobbing me and yelling, "Hey, you, you're the man. Please sign this piece of paper. Take my shirt!" Ever notice that the shirt is always triple extra-large? You try to shrink it, but you realize that no human could possibly wear this shirt. What a scam.

SO THERE WAS all this controversy about the presidential election and the so-called butterfly ballot where a bunch of people messed up and voted for the wrong guy. Everyone was upset about how such a ballot could have been used. Has anyone used an ATM on campus lately? The arrows on the screen never point directly to any of the buttons—it's confusing as hell! Forget choosing the president—I want to know if I'm taking out 10 bucks or 10,000 bucks!

AND I LOVE when the ATM asks if you will accept some exorbitant fee for your transaction. Well, let me see here. I'm completely broke, my student loan bills are overdue, I owe my buddy twenty bucks, I haven't eaten in two days, I haven't even bought my textbooks yet, and the one ATM in the whole country that doesn't charge me fees is two hundred miles away in my hometown. Yes, I'll pay the damn fee, I'm desperate! And have you ever noticed that whatever your receipt says your balance is, it's never what you expected it to be?

WHY DOESN'T THE guy at the campus deli counter ever cut my sandwich all the way in half? He always leaves that little piece attached so I have to pull it apart and ruin the sandwich. All I'm asking for is a clean cut here.

ONE OF THE best days of my college career was when, during my sophomore year, Penn beat Harvard in football to capture the Ivy League championship. At Penn we have a tradition that goes beyond the usual tearing down of the goalposts. After we tear them down, we are supposed to carry them out of the stadium—only this year they locked the stadium gates on us. So we used the uprights as a battering ram to knock down the gate, carried the goalposts through campus, out into the middle of Philadelphia, onto the expressway, and then threw them in the river. When the gate was broken down, I fell and started to get trampled by the crowd. My friend grabbed me and yelled, "I'm not going to let you die here!" It was awesome.

LATER THAT YEAR, Penn beat Princeton in basketball to win the Ivy League Championship and a spot in the NCAA Tournament. My friends and I traveled to Princeton, one of the worst places on earth, to watch the game. At the arena, Princeton graciously sat us so far from the court I couldn't even tell which team was scoring. However, upon winning the title we stormed the court. Unfortunately, I lost my balance, fell, and was trampled by a few hundred people. I hurt my shoulder pretty badly, but my pain was lessened when I saw myself crushed on the lead story on *SportsCenter*. One day I can tell my kids that my sophomore year at Penn, I stormed a basketball court, threw goalposts into a river, got trampled twice, and made *SportsCenter*. I love college.

BECAUSE OF MY injuries from getting trampled at the basketball game, I spent the whole next day in the Student Health Center and therefore had a lot of time to think. I realized that getting hurt isn't glorious anymore like it was in high school. In high school you either got hurt playing a sport or getting into a fight, and that was pretty cool. But in college most people don't play sports or fight that much anymore. College kids only get hurt by falling when drunk, getting beaten up by bouncers at a club, or like me, getting trampled at a basketball game. Getting hurt used to be cool, but now it's kind of embarrassing.

THE STUDENT HEALTH Center has got to be one of the biggest jokes on campus. Kids would rather try to cure their illnesses on their own than waste away all day in the waiting room. When I went for my trampled shoulder, they told me to come back in three weeks to see an orthopedist. By that time, my arm would have either healed completely or fallen off! My friend had a minor procedure done at Student Health once. To test if his anesthesia had worn off, they asked him who the president of the school was. He named his tenth-grade chemistry teacher. They gave him two Advils and let him leave.

BECAUSE OF SOME unfortunate events at the University of Pennsylvania my junior year, the administration decided to make the campus dry indefinitely, meaning no parties with alcohol. Now, Penn is not a very politically active campus. When a Chinese leader, accused of human rights violations, came to speak on campus, there was barely a peep from the students. When it was discovered that clothing with the school logo on it might be made in sweatshops, no one really cared. But when they tried to take our beer away, we fought like never before, marching one thousand strong to the center of campus for a protest rally that eventually ended the dry policy. It just goes to show what college students really care about these days.

VIDEO-STORE ARGUMENTS really bother me. Let's say it's a slow night on campus so you decide to stay in and rent a movie. You're in the video store and finally pick one out and your friend says, "Oh, don't get that, it was on TV last week." I hate when people say that. Who cares? Is it on TV right now? No? Good, then let's rent it.

HOW NICE IS campus when it's sunny out? Everyone is outside, kids are lying out on the grass and walking their dogs. I love when tours of prospective students come around and they're all like, "Wow, is it always like this?" I just want to say, "Yeah, except from October to March when it's cold and miserable and no one leaves the house."

I ALWAYS GET pissed off when I call the registrar's office to ask a question. The woman there always treats me like an idiot when she's giving me information. She'll be like, "OK, are you ready? Here it is: C as in Charlie, E as in Elephant, P as in Paul . . ." I'm like, how about S as in Shut the hell up, I can understand you!

EVER NOTICE THAT half of all water fountains on campus don't work?

IF YOU'RE UP early enough on a Sunday morning at any college across the country, you're bound to see a phenomenon known as the "walk of shame." The walk of shame, as every college kid knows, occurs when a guy and a girl hook up, and then the next morning one of them has to trudge home wearing the same thing they wore the night before. Some people are very embarrassed when they have to "walk." Me, I don't really mind it so much. I think of it more as a walk of triumph.

PENN HAS AN obsession with naked men. If you get shut out in Beer Pong, you have to run naked. The night before the first economics exam, if you think you're going to fail, you streak across the Quad. And on the day of the first snowfall, kids run naked too. I'm not sure where these traditions came from, but I think it's sexist that men are the only ones participating. It's only right that the girls should have to run naked too. Say, every other Tuesday.

THE DRY CLEANERS on campus suck. They're the worst. I wear a pair of khakis, I get some dirt on them, so I take them to the dry cleaners. You know what the guy says to me? "I don't know if we can get this out." What do you mean, you don't know if you can get this out? It's dirt! What purpose do you serve? I bring in dirty pants and you give me back pants that are still dirty, folded nicely on a hanger with a plastic bag? What kind of crap is that? You're the goddamn dry cleaners! Get it wet if you have to!

GRAD STUDENTS ARE funny. I was talking to my friend who goes to Penn Law, and he told me a story about how all the law students were playing a game of flag football when two of the guys collided. One was hurt pretty badly. While the EMS guy helped the injured student, he joked, "Hey, aren't you guys medical students? You should know how to do this." To which one of the guys replied, "Actually, we're law students. And we just took a class on malpractice, so I'd be very careful if I were you."

ONE YEAR THE University of Pennsylvania felt very gracious. They gave us Friday off for Fall Break. Friday? What kind of crap is that? What college kid has class on Friday? Next thing you know Spring Break will be a long weekend.

THIS IS A little embarrassing, but what the hell. At one point in the semester I was feeling a bit, well, irregular. I emailed my mom to ask her what I should do. She wrote me back with some advice as to how I could, um, get things flowing a little better. As I read the email, I started to notice that everyone in the computer lab was looking at me and snickering. I looked up and saw that my computer was hooked up to a huge screen that was projecting my email in front of the whole lab! I couldn't show my face on campus for weeks after that.

CHAPTER FOUR

Life
in the
Classroom

In between drinking and sleeping, college students have little time to squeeze in the necessary evil known as "going to class." You see, college students don't really understand the meaning of the word "optional," as in "class is optional." We're sitting around freshman year, and an upperclassman or even a professor will say, "You know, class is optional." And we'll be like, "Hey, doesn't 'optional' mean I don't have to go?" And so we almost never do.

Lately, it seems like colleges are actually encouraging kids *not* to go to class. We've got classes on tape, classes on the Internet, we can buy the notes, it's getting pretty ridiculous. It's gotten to the point where you're probably better off skipping all your classes and catching up on your sleep instead. And I love when the professor hands out all the notes and slides for the class on the first day. Are you kidding me? At that point, I usually raise my hand and ask when the midterm is, because I know that's the next time I'm showing up.

When we do go to class, however, it's always an

interesting experience because the classroom itself is like a whole other world. You're sitting in the back of a huge lecture hall in these weird, constantly broken swivel chairs. You can barely stay awake, you're still drunk from the night before, and some crazy professor with chalk all over him is going on and on about marginal demand or something. But just before you nod off completely, you hear the professor utter those wonderful words, "Remember, this assignment is *optional,*" and you fall asleep with a smile on your face.

TAKING EXAMS IN college is easy. Figuring out the curve is the hard part. I have no idea how the curve works. How do I get a 25 and get an A? How do I get a 95 and get a C? Do you ever get the feeling that the curve is just one big conspiracy against you? Like before you got to class the professor and everybody else figured out the exact mean and standard deviation that would screw you the most? Those bastards.

IT'S AMAZING TO hear the stupid things that come out of some people's mouths in the classroom. In one class we were discussing the Year 2000 problem in which some computers weren't able to recognize the date change. My friend Harlan raised his hand and said, "I don't understand the problem—what did they do in the year 1900?" The kid goes to an Ivy League school and he's still an idiot.

I HAVE DISCOVERED the best spectator sport: watching kids fall asleep in class. It's hilarious! You know, first their eyes start to close, then their head falls down, then it nods back up again, then down again, then up again. Pretty soon everyone in the class is fixated on this poor guy who can't keep his eyes open. Yeah, it's always funny until it's you. Then it's like, "Why the hell didn't you guys wake me up?"

HAVE YOU EVER noticed that when you're the one falling asleep in class there is absolutely nothing that can keep you awake? You're sitting in the most uncomfortable chair with the professor blabbing on and on and you're using your books as a pillow and the one thing in the whole world you want to do right then is go to sleep. But when class is finally over, you go home and lie in your wonderfully comfortable bed and what happens? You can't fall asleep!

IN SOME WAYS, going to class is like Sea World. If you choose to sit in the first seven or eight rows, you know you are going to get called on. That's the Splash Zone, because you have to pay attention or else you'll get soaked. Everyone in the other rows is just sitting back and eating popcorn because they know they'll never have to answer any questions.

THE WORST ARE Friday morning classes. You can just feel the collective hangover in the air. No one speaks, everyone is yawning. Occasionally, you see the guy in the back shaking his head and muttering to himself, probably remembering something dumb he did the night before when he was bombed.

WHY DO PROFESSORS hand out a syllabus on the first day of class that already has reading assigned for that day? For those of you not yet in college, a syllabus basically outlines the semester for a class. It helps you plan which classes you are going to skip, what assignments you are going to blow off, and the date of the final exam, the day before which is when you should buy the textbook.

HOW CAN PROFESSORS be so boring? Aren't there any screening processes? Do they just pick these guys off the streets and say, "Hey, want to be a college professor?" I swear I have that guy from *Ferris Bueller's Day Off* for at least three classes.

IN REALITY, IT'S actually pretty difficult to become a college professor. First, you have to get your Bachelor's degree. Then, you have to go back to school to get a Master's. After that you have to go to school for another couple of years, write a hundred-page thesis, and get your Ph.D. Even then you still have to get your work published in order to get hired. So what happens after these professors go through all those years of school and get all those degrees? They lose the ability to realize that they have chalk all over their face, hands, and pants while lecturing in front of three hundred students. You can tell every place your professor scratches because he leaves a trail of chalk dust and doesn't have a clue. And of course, no student is going to stand up and tell him he looks ridiculous, so the chalkiness continues.

I DON'T UNDERSTAND why my professors still can't work the audiovisual equipment in the classrooms. Trying to watch a video becomes a half-hour ordeal because this jerk with seven Ph.D.'s can't figure out the VCR. Just hit PLAY you idiot!

I THINK IT'S a little messed up that some professors make their students buy a book that they wrote for the class they are teaching. I wonder even more when the professor teaches the textbook out of order. How can you disagree with the order of the book? You wrote it!

I HATE THOSE kids who overreact in class when the professor accidentally makes that screeching sound on the blackboard. Does it really bother you that much? Girls are screaming and crying and running out of the room. What the hell is wrong with you? It's just a sound, quit acting like it's the end of the world!

ISN'T IT FUNNY how kids avoid sitting in the first few rows of a lecture hall? It'll be the professor, twelve empty rows, and then the entire rest of the class jammed in the back. Kids walk in late, see there are no seats in the back, and just leave. No one wants to sit near the Splash Zone, I guess.

COLLEGE KIDS LOVE to brag about how little class they go to. A typical exchange:

"When was the last time you went to class?"

"Oh, I haven't gone since the midterm."

"Oh yeah, well I skipped the midterm, I haven't been there since the first day."

"Dude, I've never been there. If all you had to do for the final exam was pick out a picture of the professor, I'd fail!"

ISN'T IT THE worst when you drop your pen in class and it lands just out of reach? First you try to stretch and reach it without getting up. Then you try to drag it with your feet, but that doesn't work either so you end up crawling on the floor like an idiot while everyone else in class is wondering what the hell you're doing.

DON'T YOU LOVE trying to sneak out of a class early? You gather all your books so that they can be easily grabbed and you move to the edge of your seat. You scan the aisles to see if there are any backpacks or sleeping kids that might block your path to the exit. Then you wait for just the right moment when the professor turns his back and starts to write on the board. It's your chance. You grab your books and tiptoe to the door, making sure to close it very quietly so as not to get the professor's attention. You made it! Freedom! On to Happy Hour at the bar! I love college.

HAS THIS EVER happened to you? You're wearing a bunch of layers because it's pretty cold outside. You're sitting in class and you start to get a little warm so you take off your sweatshirt, only the shirt you're wearing under it comes off as well so now you're sitting in class half naked and you can't even tell that everyone is wondering what the hell you're doing because all your clothes are inside-out around your head.

IS IT OK to take the book you are reading in class to the bathroom with you? Once, I walked out of poly sci with the big-ass textbook under my arm. When I came back ten minutes later, everyone was giving me looks. I mean, if you have to read something while on the can, it might as well be relevant to the class you're missing, right?

MY FRIEND JEREMY had an interesting experience with a professor once. He went to the professor's office hours to argue for more points on a paper he had just gotten back. The professor read the paper, mulled it over for a minute, and then said, "You know what? This paper is actually worse than I first thought. I'm going to lower your grade," and sent my friend on his way. What a sucker.

I TOOK THIS COURSE once where the professor smoked a pipe during class. Kind of strange, but not really a big deal, right? But listen to this—he even lets kids smoke cigarettes during class! I am not kidding. Everyone in the back was lighting up. How ridiculous is that? The only good thing is that with all the smoke in the room, no one even noticed when I left to go to the bathroom carrying the textbook!

I LOVE WHEN the professor says, "OK, this next part is not going to be on the exam but I think you should know it anyway." She might as well say, "OK, for the next fifteen minutes don't pay attention at all, just do the crossword puzzle and play Snake on your cell phone while I ramble on," because that's what we're going to do anyway.

TEACHING ASSISTANTS ARE such a joke. When was the last time a TA was actually helpful? Never! That's because the only requirements to become one are that they took the class three years ago with a different professor and different material and they didn't fail. One time I went to see a TA, and she actually charged me because I went to see her outside of office hours! Speaking of office hours, they should just rename them "a waste of my time." Basically, you go to see a TA, spend an hour trying to explain to him what you don't understand, and then another hour trying to explain to him that he's just confusing you further before you get up and leave and say to yourself, "Damn, that was a waste of my time."

EVER NOTICE THAT kids will vote to end a review session early no matter how important it is? The professor will say, "So we're going to cover everything that is going to be on the exam tomorrow, and it's some pretty complicated stuff, but if you guys want, we can wrap up now," and the place empties out in like two seconds.

MY RUSSIAN LITERATURE professor (hey, it was an easy A) was hilarious. This guy knew everything about Russia but had no common sense. One day he was taking attendance and was saying, with this thick accent, "Marecat? Marecat? Is Marecat here?" We're all looking around wondering what the hell he is talking about, and then one girl hesitantly asks, "Do you mean Mary Kate? That's me." And he goes, "Oh, Mary Kate . . . like the name?"

THERE IS NOTHING that college students look forward to more than the last day of classes. But what is with this clapping at the end of the semester? At Penn, on the last day of class, if the professor was halfway decent, he'd get an ovation. Shouldn't the students be getting the applause? We're the ones that took your psychotic tests and dragged ourselves to your 9 A.M. classes and spent our precious beer money on the $100 textbook that you wrote and made us buy but that didn't even follow your syllabus that sucked anyway. Clap for us, damnit!

Greek

Life

Greek life was a very important part of my college experience. As a freshman, I rushed and pledged Zeta Beta Tau. As a sophomore, I lived in the ZBT house. And as a junior and senior, I served as Rush Chair, helping to recruit a new generation of binge-drinking, trouble-making, Beer Pong–playing young men into the fraternity. Though my house has been around for a hundred years, I definitely think I made my mark on the fraternity. (At the very least I left a vomit stain on the carpet in the chapter room.)

Greek life creates an interesting dynamic on campus because half the kids are in a frat or sorority and half aren't. The Independents are repulsed by the Greeks' crude and vile behavior. The Greeks barely acknowledge the Independents' existence. In the end, however, both groups live happily together because without the Greeks there would be no parties, but without the Independents there would be no one at the parties.

Many years from now I will be able to return to Penn's campus and show my kids the ZBT house where I drank away most of my college career. And when my son eventually goes away to college himself and asks if he should go Greek or stay Independent, I will advise him in the proper direction. After all, I will always be a Rush Chair at heart.

ONE OF MY favorite times of year at college is Rush, which is when the fraternities and sororities decide who they will take into their new pledge classes. Rush goes a little something like this: The freshmen girls put on their finest black pants and have fake conversations with sorority girls they will eventually backstab. Later, the sororities will utilize the accurate process of Scantron bubble sheets to determine which girls are best suited for their house. Meanwhile, the freshmen guys learn that free beer does taste better and get so wasted they don't even remember which frat boys they were talking to. Later, the frat boys will attempt to figure out which guys they want even though they were so bombed they didn't even know Rush was going on in the first place. It sure is a good thing that the next three years of a person's social life are determined in such an efficient manner.

AS A FRESHMAN, Rush was a great experience for me. I got to meet a lot of cool people, saw a bunch of strippers, and got really drunk for free. Probably the best parts were going to the lame frats early and eating all the free food before the people who were actually interested showed up. In the end, I decided to choose Zeta Beta Tau. After all, they had the most free beer and the hottest strippers!

MY FAVORITE RUSH event is called the Back Nine. Now don't get me wrong, there was absolutely no golf involved. Basically, each hole is a different off-campus apartment with different liquor. For instance, at one hole hot chicks pour tequila into the freshmen's mouths before they get hurled against a padded wall. At another hole we drop a forty-foot funnel down a stairwell, and the rushes funnel about ten beers at a time. The best part about the Back Nine is that we can keep having it every year since no one ever remembers a thing!

I THINK YOU can sum up Greek life this way: Sororities are a bunch of girls who hate each other, organized to travel in herds and fight over frat boys. Fraternities are a bunch of guys who love each other, organized to get wasted faster and cheaper and hook up with sorority girls.

FRESHMAN YEAR, MY fraternity threw a black-tie charity event. Afterward, we all came back to the dorm wasted off our rockers and pimped out in tuxedos. As we came into the Quad, we saw that someone had thrown a shoe up onto one of the ledges, about twenty feet up. So my friend Dave gets the brilliant idea to scale the wall and get the shoe down. But then he falls off the wall and cracks his head on the cement. So we have to take him to the hospital. We're there for about twenty minutes when another group of pledges comes into the emergency room, and one of them, Joey, has his hand wrapped in a towel. In a completely unrelated fit of drunken stupidity, this kid smashed his hand through a window. So here we are, it's four in the morning, and twenty of my best friends and I are all wearing tuxedos in the emergency room, waiting for our friends to get stitched up and chugging beers with the security guards. It was one of the best nights of the year.

IT WAS PRETTY funny trying to explain Greek life to Europeans went I went abroad. They were like, "So let me get this straight. First they treat you like kings and selectively choose who gets to join? Then you are treated like a slave for four months and made to eat cat food and puke on demand? Then you live in a giant house with unlimited beer and slutty girls who come over all the time?" "Yeah, that's pretty much it," I said. And they're like, "Well . . . how can I sign up for this fraternity?"

LIVING IN A fraternity house, which I did as a sophomore, does have its luxuries. For instance, we have our own cook and all the bathrooms are men's. It occurred to me that this may be the only time in my life when I will be able to get bacon-egg-and-cheese sandwiches on demand and also piss in urinals. Ah, the simple pleasures of Greek life.

SOPHOMORE YEAR, THOUGH, I became one of those kids who never left the fraternity house. Why would I when I have everything I need—food, beer, and girls—right under one roof? The place is like a supermarket, a bar, and a whorehouse all rolled into one. So basically it's heaven.

I LOVE WHEN my frat throws its annual Halloween house party. That's because I've noticed that Halloween is an excuse for chicks to come to parties dressed as whores for no reason. They wear these little tiny skirts and high heels and all this makeup and look just like hookers. But they always say they're dressed as something else: "I'm a French maid"; "I'm an exotic dancer." Even if they're dressed like something unrelated, like a cowgirl, they still look like whores, wearing like a bikini top and boots and nothing else. Who do they think they're kidding?

GREEK LIFE DOES come full circle sometimes. Less than two years after puking my brains out at the forty-foot funnel during the Back Nine Rush event, I moved into that off-campus apartment and it became my job to devastate young freshmen livers. A week after the Back Nine my senior year, the keg with the huge funnel tied to it was still on the fourth floor, floating in pure nastiness. I'm in the bathroom when I hear a yell, a loud bang, and then a scream of pain. It seems that my friend Dave (yes, the same one who fell off the ledge three years earlier), in a momentary lapse of common sense, decided to try to swing Tarzan-style from the funnel across the stairwell. Unfortunately, the keg flipped over and dropped him a full floor before the funnel caught the floor grate. Of course, the keg tub tipped over, pouring about twenty gallons of stank beer and vomit onto my hanging friend. He ran out of the house yelling, "My skin, it's burning my skin!" I love college.

I'D LIKE TO address for a moment the fact that some people have been telling me that it is disrespectful to refer to my fraternity as a "frat." That's the dumbest thing I have ever heard. I'm a frat boy, I live in a frat house, and I go to frat parties. The whole point of fraternities is not to be politically correct, so quit your nitpicking, relax, have a beer, and stop complaining.

FRAT BOYS GET a bad rap. They say we're crude and irresponsible. Which, I guess, we are. But we're also creative in our crudeness and irresponsibility. Occasionally, we'll have mixers with a sorority at the fraternity house. We buy a couple of cases of cheap two-dollar vodka and have our pledges pour it into empty bottles of Ketel One. The girls come over and they're like, "Hey, these guys are high-class, look at that expensive vodka!" If they only knew . . .

BEING A PART of the Greek system means going to a lot of mixers, date parties, semiformals, and formals— all names dreamt up by sorority chicks. Before every event we're always all running around the frat house asking, "Wait, is this a formal mixer? A semiformal date party? Do I have to wear a tie?" Eventually, someone needs to call the sorority house to ask whether or not we're allowed to wear jeans.

OF COURSE, WITH all these date parties and formals, a frat boy is constantly trying to find a date. For one party my friend was so desperate that he actually called an escort service, but it was a bit too pricey for his needs. But for all this anxiety, I think my buddy Jay had it right when he said, "It's not who you take but who you take home with you that counts." Couldn't have said it better myself.

WHILE GREEK LIFE is an important part of the social scene at college, it certainly isn't the end of the world if you are not in a house. But for some reason I find that girls need to justify to me why they are not in a sorority. I'll say, "Hey, Danielle, are you going to the Tri-Delt date party tonight?" And she'll respond, "Actually, I'm not in a sorority. Freshman year I really wanted to concentrate on my studies and didn't have time for Rush or pledging. And I don't want to have to be defined by what house I'm in. I'm my own person and I'm fine with that, and it doesn't bother me at all that I'm not part of one of these exclusive organizations." Um, I guess that's a no.

I THINK IT'S pretty absurd how fraternities ignore the liquor laws on campus. I mean, they throw huge parties at the fraternity house, where all the underage sophomores live. They hand out flyers for the party in the freshmen dorms. They might as well hire high school kids to check IDs at the door—and pay them in whiskey!

THERE IS ONE conversation about Greek life that always bothers me. I'll be talking to someone and they'll ask me what frat I'm in. So I tell them I'm in ZBT. Then they ask me, "Oh, do you know this brother? Do you know that brother?" I know every brother, you moron, I'm *in* the fraternity!

MOST OF MY time spent in the fraternity house—and in fact, most of my time at college in general—revolved around a drinking game called Beer Pong. Just to get a little terminology straight here, Beer Pong is played with paddles, a ball, and two cups on either side, as opposed to Beirut, which involves many more cups and no paddles. Many people get confused between the two, but at Penn, the game of choice is Pong. In my fraternity, if your team gets shut out 11 to 0, you have to run naked (or "streak") to a certain landmark and back, rain or shine. Every once in a while a couple of hapless freshmen wander into the house and enter into a game versus some highly skilled seniors. There's nothing like a freshman's face when he's down 10 to 0, returning serve, with an entire fraternity house screaming, "Streak, streak, streak!" Because you know the kid is thinking, Oh man, I thought we were playing Beirut.

Aaron Karo

EVERY FALL MY fraternity throws its annual Toga Party. The party's slogan, appropriately enough, is "Come in Your Sheets!" I just love watching a house full of freshmen, drunk out of their heads, wearing nothing but extra-long twin sheets. It's amazing how in college this kind of social behavior is not only condoned, but actually encouraged. Sometimes, I'll observe the party and think to myself, in four years, all these people will graduate with Ivy League degrees, won't know a Roman from a Greek, but will be able to take a piss while wasted and wearing a toga.

THE ONLY PROBLEM with my frat house is that we have the worst showers ever. If anyone in the whole house flushes, the showers start alternating from freezing cold to thermonuclear hot every thirty seconds. And when it gets hot, you have to do that little shower dance. You know what I'm talking about—you arch your back to avoid the burning water and hop on the balls of your feet to the corner of the shower. Then you have to acrobatically reach your hand around the scorching stream and try to get to the knob without burning off any sexual organs!

ONE OF THE great benefits of belonging to a fraternity is the handing down of exams and homework assignments from the older brothers to the younger ones. Of course, over the years, many professors have gotten wind of our little schemes. In one of my classes, a kid, obviously non-Greek, raised his hand and asked the professor if there were any old tests or papers from the class available to study from. The professor replied, "Well, I don't know—are you in fraternity?"

THIS GUY IN my fraternity, Cliff, was ranked number one in the country in fencing and went to the Olympics in Sydney in 2000. The thing is, I was definitely excited for the kid, but every time we started talking about him, I kind of got depressed. I mean, talk about motivation, this kid went to the Olympics and my loftiest goal was to win my frat's Beer Pong championship!

WHY DO GIRLS who deactivate from their sorority act like they were never in a sorority to begin with? I'll be like, "Oh, hey, Jen, I just saw some of your pledges." And she'll say, "I don't know what you're talking about, I'm not in a sorority." Damnit, you know what I mean! Just remember, girls, once a sorority chick, always a sorority chick. There's no going back!

THE SORORITIES AT Penn sometimes have mixers with the Penn Law School. How hilarious is that? I can just imagine a bunch of dirty old third-year law students hitting on wasted eighteen-year-old sorority chicks. It's ironic, because you'd think the law students would realize what they're doing is barely legal!

FRATERNITIES ARE BEING cracked down on all across the country. Penn itself has been anything but supportive of our existence. One of the main reasons that colleges want to get rid of frats is the problem of excessive drinking. They say fraternities cause their members to become binge drinkers. What—do they think I never drank excessively before I joined a frat? It's not like we were all standing around after pledging being like, "OK, we're in the fraternity, now what do we do? Wait, is that a beer can over there? Hey, let's binge drink!"

OF COURSE, THE campus crackdown on fraternities does have some humorous consequences for the affected brothers. My buddy Eric, although I advised him not to, insisted on getting his fraternity's symbol branded on his shoulder. Two months later his house was shut down and kicked off campus. I couldn't stop laughing.

WHEN I WAS at Dartmouth visiting my sister, Caryn, I was kind of taken aback by the fact that all there is to do there is hang out at fraternity houses and play Beer Pong. I figured it must be pretty boring to go to school in the middle of nowhere. Then I thought, wait a minute, I go to school in Philadelphia, which has tons of clubs and bars, and what do I do every night? Hang out at my fraternity house and play Pong.

I LOVE MY frat brothers. But when I look at my friend who is pre-med, I think, I saw this drunken fool throw up on himself last night—there is no way I would ever let him operate on me! Then I look at my buddy who is pre-law and think, This kid gets wasted and breaks stuff all the time—I would never let him represent me in court! So I guess that is what fraternities are really all about: getting wasted, meeting your best friends, and knowing who *not* to call later in life when you need a doctor or a lawyer!

CHAPTER SIX

The Cast of Characters

College would not be the same without Room Scavengers, Highlighters, People from Los Angeles, Oversleepers, Kids with Cars, High School Football Players, Nodders, Slow Walkers, Pre-med Kids, Secret Studiers, Early Planners, Big-Backpack People, Shady Backpack People, Lazy Kids, Flash-Card Makers, Kids Who Can't Resist Peer Pressure, the Old Guy, Friends Afraid to Be Alone, Kids Without a Computer, Front-Row Sitters, Kids Who Love College Football, Constant Celebrators, Summer Campers, Kids Who Write Down Everything, Glowstick Kids, Not the Domino's Guy, Whisperers, Underdressers, and Early Finals Finishers, to name a few.

College campuses are full of some of the weirdest, most hilarious, and most annoying people in the world. What's amazing is that all these people went through the same application process that you did. They wrote essays and had interviews just like you did. They were carefully selected from a pool of thousands of people, just like you were. You start thinking to yourself, Am I one of them?

When it comes down to it, though, how much fun you have in college is really determined by who's along on the journey with you. Your friends, your classmates, the kids you see on campus, they're all a part of it. If college were a movie, this would be the cast of characters. And don't worry—you're here too.

EVERYONE HAS THAT friend who will always respond to peer pressure. If no one else will go out boozing with you, you always know that you can turn to him. And it's so easy too:

> **You: Yo, Jon, let's go out and get hammered.**
>
> **Jon: No, man, I have a test tomorrow and I haven't even started studying.**
>
> **You: C'mon, dude, you can study in the morning.**

Jon: No way, dude, the test is at nine A.M.

You: But it's your favorite! Dollar beers!

Jon: OK, OK, let me get my ID, I'll study at the bar if I have to.

Works every time!

I'M A NEW YORKER, born and raised. So when I got to college, there were certain kids I never understood. Namely, kids from the West Coast. Penn must have done some extra recruiting there or something because the campus was overrun with these guys. It's funny because kids from the West Coast stick out like a sore thumb at a college in the Northeast. You want to know how you can spot a college kid from Los Angeles? They're always talking about Los Angeles: "Oh, the weather is great, there's no humidity, my dad's this big-time agent, I saw this movie star in the deli, Kobe was dope last night, blah, blah, blah." No one cares—shut up and go home!

DO YOU HAVE that friend who won't do anything alone? I lived with this one guy, Dan, who absolutely had to be accompanied by someone wherever he went:

"Karo, yo, dude, you going to class? Wait up." "Hey, Karo, I'm gonna get a haircut, come with?" "Karo, I'm going to the dry cleaners, take a walk with me?" I'm like, "Dude, the dry cleaners is two doors down from our house—what, do you need me to hold your hand?"

UNLIKE MANY OF my friends, I wasn't a big fan of taking naps before I went out partying for the night. I figured, well, I already slept until 4 P.M., what do I need a nap for? I was also really scared of sleeping through the whole night. You know, there's always that one kid who takes a power nap at 8 P.M. and then stumbles into the party at 2 A.M. like, "Dude, I just woke up." No one wants to be that guy.

EVERYONE LOVES THAT kid who brings his car to campus. However, I can't stand people who talk about their cars in code. They'll be like, "Yeah I drive a 525i but the other day I saw the new A4 Turbo, which looks just like the VX3 but it's a little faster than the 750." What the hell are you talking about?

HAVE YOU SEEN these kids on campus who live in

the football-player parallel universe? They're the ones who were big-time players in high school but are too small or not good enough to play in college. But they still wear their high school jersey and letter jacket and hat because in their mind they're still playing football. It's actually pretty sad.

SPEAKING OF FOOTBALL, what's with kids who go to college at big-time football schools? All they talk about is sports. I'm talking to my friend Claudio who goes to Michigan, and I ask him, "How's the weather up there?" He's not even listening to me. He says, "You know we won the Rose Bowl?" I'm like, "Yes, you've told me eight times already. I don't care."

EVEN IN THIS digital day and age, everyone knows that one kid who still doesn't have a computer in his dorm room. You know, he was that guy who would roll into your room and pretend to be just stopping by, then ask if he could check his email, and the next thing you knew, he was typing a paper on your laptop. For some reason this is usually the same kid who always gives your computer a virus no matter what disk he uses, like it's in his blood or something.

WHAT ABOUT YOUR friend who always asks what is going on that night . . . at like 11 A.M.? I just woke up, I haven't spoken to anybody yet, how the hell would I know? I think there should be some type of restriction on how early you can ask about the night's festivities.

I HAVE THIS friend Adam who is so lazy he ordered the campus laundry service one year. But that's not even the lazy part. He's so lazy that he couldn't even bring himself to carry his laundry bag over to the drop-off point, so he ended up just doing it himself anyway! Now that's lazy. Of course, this is the same kid who one semester took a cab to class and back—every day!

DO YOU HAVE friends that leave their phone number on your answering machine every time they call? I have this one good friend from high school who I speak to every week or so. And every time the kid calls me and leaves a message on my machine, he leaves his phone number. I have your number already—what the hell is wrong with you?

THERE ARE TWO kinds of kids who really annoy me

in the classroom. The nodders and the flash-card makers. A nodder is that dork in the front of the class who doesn't ever say anything but just nods his head in approval at whatever the teacher says. Teachers like nodders because it gives them the impression that someone has a clue about what the hell they're talking about. Then there are the people who make flash cards before every single test. Even math! There are no definitions—what the hell are you quizzing yourself on? If the flash-card makers would spend more time studying and less time crafting these color-coded index cards, they would do a lot better.

THEN YOU HAVE the big-backpack people. These are the kids who walk around hunched over because they have every single book with them at all times. Sometimes their bags are so full the zipper won't even stay shut. Big-backpack people don't seem to ever be reading their books, just carrying them around. And what's with these backpacks with forty-five straps hanging off them in every direction? Do they serve a purpose? You're going to class, not climbing Mt. Everest!

MAYBE THE ONLY thing worse than big-backpack people are slow walkers. Slow walkers like to stroll leisurely side by side up the stairs right in front of you, blocking your path when you're late for class. Instead of walking by them you have to get right up behind them to try to get them to hurry up and are forced to listen to their stupid conversations about flash cards and big backpacks. Leave a lane for passing goddamnit!

DO YOU HAVE that friend that still goes away to camp every summer? What is wrong with these people? At the end of every summer you have to hear from them about camp: "Oh, my bunk was so awesome! And color war was great, we won, but it was the closest score ever!" Are you kidding me? They say it was the closest score every year! You're twenty years old, get a damn job!

I LOVE PRE-MED kids. They're just plain nuts, especially when it comes to the MCATs. Those crazy bastards won't go out for five months just to study for one test. I had to study medicine along with my pre-med friends just so I was able to administer first-aid to them when they got absolutely wrecked right after the test.

YOU KNOW WHO I hate? Whoever is at the door when you've been waiting for Domino's for an hour and a half and the doorbell rings and you get all excited and run all the way downstairs and open the door only to see some other jerk at the door and not the Domino's guy.

DO YOU HAVE a friend who's a secret studier? You know, that kid who is always so nonchalant about the test: "Oh, I'm not really worried about the exam tomorrow," or "Yeah, maybe I'll review the notes." But on test day they whip out a stack of color-coded flash cards and a fully indexed study sheet, and ace the exam. You know what's not a secret? You're a dork and a liar!

MAYBE THE ONLY life form lower than the secret studier is the front-row sitter. These guys are really easy to spot. Everyone knows that in a college classroom you have to sit as far back as possible and never sit in the first seven or eight rows, ever. But there she is, right smack in the middle of the front row. Even the professor hates front-row sitters. Because at least if everyone is in the back, he can maybe justify it and say to himself, "Oh, maybe there is just a glare in the front or something." But not with the front-row sitters there. I think the front row is kind of like the hangout for the flash-card makers, nodders, slow walkers, big-backpack people, and secret studiers. Kind of like their own little lame fraternity or something.

I LOVE THOSE kids who get wasted after they finish any minor assignment. I'm like, "Hey, Scott, why are you so wasted, it's only two P.M.?" And he'll say, "Yeah, man, I just handed in my Spanish homework, it took me like an hour and a half to do, I gotta celebrate. Let's chug a beer!" And this happens every Tuesday and Thursday.

WHAT'S WITH THESE kids who bring glowsticks to parties? They look like they're directing airport traffic.

DO YOU HAVE that friend who will only let you pay him back in beer? I'll be like, "Hey, dude, here's the ten bucks I owe you." And he'll say, "No, no, you'll just get me back at the bar." And I'll say, "Dude, I have the money now though, just take it." And he'll be like, "No, your money is no good here! I will only accept alcohol as repayment." Weird.

HOW ABOUT THOSE kids in lecture who write down

everything? Teacher puts something on the board, he writes it down. Teacher sneezes, kid makes a note of it. The kid is writing when the teacher isn't even talking! And you're sitting there thinking, Should I be writing this down?

I HATE THOSE kids who always finish their exams right at the beginning of finals week and call you up every night while you're still studying to tell you how drunk they are. Wait a minute . . . that kid is me. Oops.

YOU KNOW WHO I never understood? Kids who highlight every single line in the reading for a class. First of all, with all those yellow marks it's like bragging to anyone within a two-mile radius that you were dumb enough to analyze the entire reading. Second of all, what the hell is the point if you're just going to highlight every sentence? How does that really help?

ANOTHER STAPLE ON college campuses is, of course, the old guy. Old Guy is that guy who graduated like three years ago but still hangs out on campus. Old Guy doesn't go to grad school, he doesn't have a job, no one is quite sure what he does, but he's always around.

One thing is for certain, though, Old Guy *loves* freshmen girls.

I HATE SITTING next to that kid in class who constantly says the answer to the professor's question under his breath like he's showing off or something. He'll whisper the answer just loud enough for me to hear. If he's right, he'll give that little smirk. If he's wrong, he won't say anything. When that happens, I just want to whisper under my breath, "I guess you're not so smart after all, you moron!"

WHO ARE THOSE shady kids who wear backpacks to parties?

DO YOU HAVE that friend who is always looking to steal stuff for his dorm room? He's like an obsessed scavenger. Every time he sees a sign, he's like, "Dude, that would look awesome in my room! Keep an eye out while I go rip it down."

I LOVE THOSE kids who have to be the first to wear shorts and a T-shirt when the weather starts to get warmer. You know, on that day when it's just a little bit sunnier, but definitely still too cold to wear shorts, there are always kids who have to wear sandals, shorts, a tank top, and sunglasses. And they'll never admit they're cold when you know they're freezing. Where are these kids from? Yup, you guessed it. Los Angeles.

CHAPTER SEVEN

Home

Sweet

Home

The only bad part about going away to college is that, eventually, you have to come back home. Just when you think you're getting into a groove at college— you're getting some good grades, you're hooking up, things are going well—Bam! Thanksgiving break comes along and you're back at home sweet home. And that means dealing with your parents. It's funny, because I know my parents went to college. Sure it was a long, long, long time ago, but they still went. Yet they seem to be completely oblivious as to what actually happens on campus. How can this be?

The thing with parents is that you have to learn how to manage them. If you think you're going to go off to college, collect your monthly check, and then completely ignore your mom and dad, you have another think coming. They need to know what's going on. So tell them what they want to hear. When you go out to a concert and get wasted, tell them you went to a "show." When you bomb your midterms but get an A on a homework assignment that counts for 1 percent of your grade, play up the A. Make them proud. After all, half the time they have no idea what the hell you're talking about anyway.

Twenty-five years from now when my children go off to school, will I forget what college life is really like? Will I actually believe that all the money I am sending to my kids is going toward books? Will I be under the impression that the dorms are well supervised and orderly? I can imagine that one day I'll be talking to my son at college and I will yell at him for partying too much. And you know what he'll say? "Dad, I learned it from reading your book." Oops.

AT NO OTHER time does a college kid's life change as dramatically as it does during winter break. At school, there are parties, booze, girls everywhere, you're out, you're back, you're on the move. Then the end of December rolls around and next thing you know you're on the couch for three weeks straight watching *Real World* reruns. I always think, Where did all the girls and booze go? Shoveling snow becomes my most exciting activity. Remember in high school when you always complained that there was nothing to do in your town? You didn't have a car, you weren't twenty-one, and you had a curfew. It sucked. So now I have a car, I'm twenty-one, I have no curfew, and guess what? There's still nothing to do.

BREAK FROM SCHOOL is always time for "appointments." You get your hair cut, you go to the dentist, maybe even visit the doctor. That's because you get home and your parents are like, "Oh my God, you look terrible! I'm making you some appointments." I never understood the whole dentist thing. He's always like, "Well, you have some inflammation of your gum line, it looks a little irritated." Well it wouldn't be like that if you didn't keep poking me with that damn metal hook!

GOING HOME TO visit for a weekend is always an experience. You go home with that attitude like, "My parents better not try to control me! I'll do whatever the hell I want!" An hour later I was taking out the garbage and washing the dishes. I guess when I said my parents couldn't control me, I didn't realize that they do control the car, the house, the money . . .

OF COURSE, WHEN you're a college student, whether you're at school or on break, your parents are always there no matter what. Whether via phone, email, or personal visits, they're there. The first time my parents visited, I almost got in big trouble, stemming from the fact that I have no idea at all how to do laundry. I asked my dad if I could get the campus laundry service and he said something like, "Be a man and wash your own underwear!" That alone confused the hell out of me. Anyway, I went behind their backs and ordered the laundry service. Little did I know that when my mom came to visit I would have to take a quiz on the laundry room: "How much bleach do you use, do you need more quarters, do you have enough Static Guard?" I had no idea; I just bullshitted with her for twenty minutes until I managed to change the subject to my latest dentist appointment.

COLLEGE KIDS ARE pretty busy, you know, with all the classes we have to squeeze in between binge drinking and sleeping. So sometimes we forget to call home. About every two weeks, in colleges across the nation, kids come home to this message on their answering machine: "Hi, it's Mom, just wanted to see how you were doing. We haven't heard your voice in a while.

Please call us. Things are going well here at home. Your sister got an A on her math test. But we miss you. If you can find the time, please give us a call. Remember, Dad's birthday is on Saturday. Remember to call him. But please try to call before then. Please. We miss you. Call us. Love you—Mom. And please call home!"

EVERY ONCE IN a while when I'm home for break, I'll visit my old high school, good old Plainview JFK. Now there's a depressing experience. All the teachers look the same and they're all doing exactly the same thing. And when did everyone start dressing like total dirtbags? It's almost like my class graduated and the rest of the school got left back. But the freshmen girls looked pretty nice. Oh man, did I just say that?

BEING AROUND MY old high school made me realize the essential difference in the mentalities between high school kids and college kids. In high school, if you had to get up really early the next morning, you just went to bed early the night before. But in college, if you have to get up really early the next morning you stay up all night . . . and get wasted!

DURING THANKSGIVING BREAK of my freshman year, I played in an alumni soccer game at my old high school. My graduating class played the current varsity squad. My team was sad. I have never seen such a group of finely honed athletes degenerate into a bunch of fat, slow, beer-bellied slobs in such a short time, but I guess college will do that to you. We were winning in the first half until we ran out of steam and got crushed. Then my team did what we still knew we could do best—we went out and hit the bar hard.

EVER NOTICE THAT in high school the school year sucked and the summer ruled, but in college the summer sucks and school is awesome?

IT'S IRONIC HOW when you were in high school your parents said they didn't care what other kids did: "But Mom, Seth's parents let him go out on a school night!" The response: "I don't care what Seth does, you're not going anywhere." But in college, it's reversed: "Yeah, Mom, I'm not sure what I'm going to do after graduation." The response: "Why the hell can't you get a good job like Seth?"

I THINK THAT talking to your parents about an event

that happened in college is a lot like writing a paper, because they never understand what the hell you're talking about. You know, first you need to introduce the story, give a little background. Then you need to give your thesis statement and say exactly what happened, and use a lot of examples. Then you need a conclusion where you summarize the whole thing. And the funny part is that after you're done with all that you always know that they didn't follow your story at all because their first question is completely off the topic. You failed your paper.

HOW COME WHEN I go home for break I suddenly become "errand boy?" It's like my parents saved every single thing they had to do for when I came home. I walk in the door and there's no "Welcome home, son!" It's more like, "OK, we need milk, get the car washed, pick up your sister, and mow the lawn." Who the hell does this stuff when I'm gone?

ISN'T IT FUNNY how you can't show your parents any of the pictures that you took at school because you're wasted in all of them? When your parents ask you for pictures, you always have to be like, "Um, they're not developed yet" or "Oh, I left them at school, but they weren't good anyway." Meanwhile you have a stack of panoramics depicting you funneling beers like it's your job. My friend Christina needed a photo for a grad school application and she had to cut her head out of a picture of her holding a drink in each hand and use that because it was the soberest picture she could find.

HAVE YOU EVER come home from college for the first time in a while, gotten in the car to go somewhere, and thought to yourself, You know what? I don't even know if I remember how to drive!

IT'S FUNNY HOW my dad, my mom, and I all have such different views about college. When my sister once drank too much and slept through an exam the next day, our reactions were so different. My dad: "Well, sometimes these things happen, but don't let it happen again." My mom: "Honey, I'm very worried about you. I think you have a drinking problem." Me: "Good work, sis! Way to step it up!"

AND WHAT ABOUT using the phone at home after living in the dorm for so long? At school I have my own line, but at home I don't. I'm picking up the phone at home like, "Yeah, what the hell do you want? Oh . . . Grandma, um, I wasn't talking to you, I swear!" Plus at home all you have to do is dial. I'm sitting there dialing 9, entering my personal access code, and I'm thinking, Why the hell isn't this working?

WHY AFTER ALL these years does my mom still think Sunday through Thursday are school nights? I'll be telling my mom about a party I'm going to, thinking nothing of it, and she'll be like, "But Aaron, it's only Tuesday." She just can't comprehend it. She doesn't understand that the only reason a college kid doesn't go out on a Tuesday is because he's too hungover from Monday night's festivities.

WHY DO I come home after being away at school and my family has changed the seating arrangements at the dinner table? And why has my room become the storage area for old clothes and my sister's shoes?

THE BEST SCENE is when you come home wrecked during break and you're forced to go in and talk to your half-sleeping parents. You try your best, but you always come away thinking you either talked really loudly to them, slurred your words, acted suspiciously, or smelled.

MY MOM'S RESPONSE to every problem is always "You drink too much." Mom, I'm not feeling well. "You drink too much." Mom, I didn't do well on my last test. "Maybe it's because you drink too much." Mom, the football team lost. "They drink too much."

THEN, OF COURSE, there's Family Weekend, you know, when your parents come up to nag you for three days straight. They might as well call the day before Hide-the-Beer Day, because all you do is empty the fridge, throw out all the bottles, and take down all the pictures of you drunk off your ass from the wall.

WHY DOES MY dad insist on wearing Penn paraphernalia every time he comes to visit? It's Family Weekend and my dad shows up wearing a Penn hat, a Penn shirt, a Penn sweatshirt, and a Penn jacket. Dad, everyone here goes to Penn!

BEING AT HOME over break made me realize why college is so great: it's basically a consequence-free environment. You don't have to drive anywhere and your parents aren't around. At home, you have to convince someone to be the designated driver when everyone's wasted and you have to remember your house alarm code when you come home trashed so you don't wake everyone up. It's almost too much of a hassle. At school you can be as loud as you want and the farthest bar is five blocks—you can just be carried home instead of having someone drive!

ISN'T IT WEIRD being home and sleeping late? At school you never really notice anything, but at home you're just waking up and your parents are coming home from work already. It makes you kind of think you're missing something.

WHY DOES THE media control my life at college? As far as my mom is concerned, whatever Barbara Walters says goes. First *20/20* had this show about binge drinking, which resulted in a two-hour discussion with my mom about my drinking habits ("Don't worry, Mom, I just nurse one beer all night"). Then *Time* magazine ran an article about excessive drinking on campus. About a week later I get an envelope in the mail from my mom. The only thing inside was a copy of the article. No money, no letter, just the article. I knew what she was thinking, though: You see, Aaron, *Time* magazine thinks you drink too much too.

WHEN IT'S WINTER at school, though, I miss my mom a lot. Why? Because she would never let me leave the house the way I dress. She'd tell me I would catch a cold, and if I didn't put on a jacket, she wouldn't let me out of the house. If I had my mom at school, maybe I wouldn't be sick all the time.

HOW COME MOMS never know their own cell phone number?

WHEN DECIDING WHAT clothes to pack for school after summer break, don't you consider every conceivable situation? Like, what if it's hailing on a partly cloudy day and I'm playing tackle football in the mud? I better take this old sweatshirt just in case! And since you end up taking basically all of your clothes, you end up wearing whatever is left the day before you leave. I couldn't even leave the house to run some last-minute errands because I had on a pair of short shorts from 1986 and those high socks with the colored stripes on them!

AFTER BEING AWAY at school for a few years, isn't it strange how your room at home is frozen in time? I went home for Thanksgiving break my senior year, and walking into my old bedroom was like walking into the past. There are posters of Kathy Ireland and Patrick Ewing (on the Knicks) lining the walls, there's a little tiny bed in the corner, and a phone with a bunch of people I never talk to anymore programmed into the memory. Here's a tip: when your parents threaten to change your room into a study after you leave for college, take them up on the offer!

SO THIS GIRL is driving me home from school one winter break, and we stop at a tollbooth on the New Jersey Turnpike. My friend is playing around and kind of flirting with the toll collector, who happens to be fairly young. We found out later that this guy wrote his phone number on the back of her toll receipt! What the hell was he thinking? That my friend would call him up and go, "Hey, this is the girl from the Honda at Exit 10. Wanna go to Bob's Big Boy sometime?"

EVEN THOUGH I'VE been in college almost four years, my parents still can't remember my friends' names. So I have to make up all these stories about them:

ME: **Yeah, Mom, so I was talking to Seth and—**

MOM: **Seth, who's Seth?**

ME: **You know Seth, he lives downstairs. [No response.] He's pre-med, likes to fish, and has a gap between his two front teeth?**

MOM: **Oh, that Seth!**

My dad has the same problem:

ME: **So, Dad, Jon is going to come over later.**

DAD: **Jon—who's Jon?**

ME: **Dad, you know Jon, he's the president of my fraternity. [No response.] He's got black spiky hair, we took him to dinner once and you got the steak and it was over-cooked.**

DAD: **Oh, Jon! Why didn't you say so in the first place?**

WHY DO WE eat so much earlier at home? At school we eat dinner at like eight or nine o'clock. When I was home for break, I was sitting down to eat at five-thirty. I was like, what the hell is going on here? I felt like I'd retired and moved to Florida. Two more weeks of that and I swear I would have been wearing blue polyester pants and playing shuffleboard.

BEING AT SCHOOL so much really does mess you up. Did you ever notice that the temperature inside your dorm is always the same, year-round? I wear short sleeves every day. I go home and it's like, since when did it get so cold in the winter? And what's with this drinking water straight from the tap? At school I have to send it through two Brita filters just to avoid getting tuberculosis!

WHY ARE THE last few days of break before you leave to go back to college the time when you run around trying to see everyone you didn't bother to hang out with the whole summer?

THE WORST PART about the grading curve is that, like me, my parents just don't understand it. Like this conversation between my Dad and me:

DAD: So, how was your test?

ME: Pretty hard, but everyone else thought it was hard too so the curve might not be that bad.

DAD: Don't worry about anyone else but yourself.

ME: I know, but if everyone else does badly, then I can still do well.

DAD: Why don't you just try harder, are you on drugs?

ME: No, Dad, it's the curve. Last test I got an A even though my grade was a 46 because of the curve.

DAD: You got a 46? We're not sending you any more money!

OF COURSE, THE one thing that parents do have a knack for is calling you at the worst times. Like when you're in your room pre-gaming with a bunch of people and everyone is loud and drinking. The phone rings, and when you find out who it is, you have to say in a very loud voice, "HI, MOM!" so that everyone in the room knows to shut up so your mom doesn't find out that you actually do drink too much.

CHAPTER EIGHT

Nightlife

Homer Simpson once said that alcohol is the cause of—and solution to—all of life's problems. Nothing sums up the typical nightly activities of a college student like that observation. High school kids can put down their share of beer. Recent alumni, they're pretty good drinkers too. But when you're in college, those are your prime drinking years. For four years we become experts on everything from fake-ID manufacturing to keg tap repair. No one can funnel, chug, or rip shots like a college kid can. Because when you get down to it, college is really all about drinking—excessively, frequently, and irresponsibly.

Excessively? I once drank so many Jack and Cokes, and got so absurdly wasted and sick, I couldn't drink Coke for three months. Frequently? In college there is no longer any such thing as a "school night"—it's drink every night until your liver gives out, you fail out of school, or you run out of money, whichever comes first. Irresponsibly? They might as well build a liquor ward at the Hospital of the University of Pennsylvania and a special cellblock at the Philadelphia Police Department to cater to all the drunken idiots who either hurt themselves or others.

Many parents may be shocked at these revelations. But guess what? They're all true. Why do you think your kid doesn't drink Coke anymore?

ISN'T THIS ONE of the greatest moments in college? You're wasted, absolutely trashed. You go back to your room and you're kind of messing around when the phone rings. It's your best friend from home. And he's wasted too! You both scream for twenty minutes about how wasted you both are and how you're going to visit each other at college and get wasted together and how you're going to get so wasted over the summer. Then you both pass out and don't remember you even spoke to each other.

I LOVE WHEN Harvard releases these studies saying something like, "One in three college students engages in so-called 'binge drinking.' 'Binge drinking' is defined as having five or more drinks in a single sitting." Hey, morons, what do you call shotgunning twelve beers after drinking half a bottle of tequila? It's hilarious to me that researchers and administrators have such a warped concept of students' drinking habits. First of all, the term "binge drinking" is redundant. How many kids do you know go out, have five beers, and then go home? None. Either we're binge drinking or we're not drinking at all. It's no surprise these researchers are from Harvard—they've probably never seen the inside of a bar.

YOU NEVER FORGET your first time. Mine was about two weeks into my freshman year. I drank too much and threw up. In my room. All over the place. I remember nothing, I just woke up in the morning and there was vomit on my dorm-room rug, much of it in my left shoe, and Rice Krispies all over the place. "The left shoe?" you ask. Well, my only guess was that the garbage can was too far away. The Rice Krispies on the other hand, I have absolutely no idea where they came from.

ONE OF THE problems that colleges across the country are trying to solve is how to get kids to stop drinking themselves into the hospital (which, on a side note, is conveniently located adjacent to the freshman dorm at Penn). Once, I was watching some medics put this wasted freshman chick into an ambulance. As she was taken away, I heard her cry, "I never even drank before!"

There you have it. The way to solve this problem is to teach drinking in high school, pure and simple.

GETTING YOUR FIRST fake ID is always a memorable experience. I remember going with my buddy to this shady kid's house on the edge of campus with a passport photo and a hundred bucks. The thing was pretty good. I only got laughed at about half of the time. I love the whole strategy of trying to get into the bar with a fake ID. You know, you have to act confident, know your home address and your zodiac sign, and pretend like you lost your wallet so you have no backup. It's funny because the longer you have an ID, the harder it is to pull off because your fake age is so high. By the time I was almost actually twenty-one my fake said I was like twenty-seven. The bouncer is like, "You're older than me!"

IT'S HILARIOUS WHEN people say that drinking is no longer fun after you turn twenty-one. Are you kidding me? It's twice as much fun now that I don't have to worry about being negged by some bouncer on a power trip! Not being able to get into a bar when all your friends can is like when you were five and not tall enough to go on the cool rides at the amusement park. The only thing that's annoying is that from the second semester of your junior year through first semester of your senior year, every weekend is someone's twenty-first birthday party. And everyone has to make such a big deal out of it: "We're going out to dinner first, then we're gonna go here, we're gonna go there, c'mon everyone's invited, I'm twenty-one!" I'm always like, "OK, I've done this twelve times already this semester. How about this? I'll show up at 1 A.M., buy you your twenty-first shot, watch you vomit, and then go home." Because there is no way they're going to remember any of it anyway!

IT'S FUNNY HOW badly guys need alcohol in order to talk to girls. My friend Joey wanted to hit on this girl in our finance class, but could not bring himself to talk to her while sober. So one day he made himself a Jack and Coke and brought it to class in a big keg cup. This thing reeked, but he drank it anyway. Only thing was, the girl didn't come to class that day, and he ended up drinking the whole thing and passing out twenty minutes later. It was a good idea, though.

SO I NOTICED they started selling the energy drink Red Bull at the commissary at school. At Penn, when you buy stuff at the commissary, you put it on your school ID card and the bill goes right to your parents. Considering I've never seen anyone drink a Red Bull without at least three shots of vodka in it, this is just another example of the university supporting students' drinking habits.

EVER NOTICE THAT when you are really drunk and you hurt yourself really badly, it's the funniest thing in the world? You'll be stumbling along and fall, and you'll be like, "Oh my God, I think I broke my ankle, how funny is this, I'm hurt really badly!" And you can't stop laughing, but the next morning your ankle is so swollen you need to get crutches. It's also funny when you're all out drinking and one of your friends hurts himself and you always ask the kid who is pre-med to take care of him. Like this kid who took two biology classes knows what the hell he's doing. If anything, the pre-med kids are even drunker because they're so stressed with organic chemistry and the MCATs.

PRE-GAMING IS the best. Pre-gaming, as every college kid knows, is when you drink large quantities of alcohol before you even go out in order to make sure you never get to a party sober. The funny thing is that college kids will pre-game no matter what. We could be going to a top-shelf open-bar party and still take a couple of shots before leaving! The best is when you pre-game a little too hard and never make it out. Those always turn out to be fun nights, although the post-game usually involves throwing up and passing out.

SPRING FLING IS this enormous annual three-day party at Penn when the campus liquor laws get ignored for the weekend and everyone goes out and gets rocked all day. Spring Fling is the time when even those kids who don't go out all year get drunk. You know that kid in your accounting class who annoys you by asking all those stupid questions? Well, now he is annoying you at a party and asking you all these stupid questions and telling you how wasted he is even though he's only had one beer. It's times like those when I wish the school would enforce the liquor laws just a little bit more.

ONE SPRING FLING, I can't really remember which one, I was particularly destroyed, to the point where I could barely stand up anymore. As I rolled around on the ground in a drunken bliss, I was quoted as saying, "Hey, I've seen more ceilings than floors today!" I love college.

A COUPLE OF TIMES during college I visited my buddy Brian at Cornell for Slope Day. Slope Day, which is basically a second-class Spring Fling, is a tradition in which everyone at Cornell emerges from the library for one day, sits on a huge hill, and gets ridiculously hammered. What I thought was funny was that there were all these emergency alcohol-response teams on the slope, not necessarily controlling the drinking, but rather waiting until people got too wasted and then swooping in with fluids and first-aid. I think the direct result of this was everyone getting even more wasted because they felt so safe. One particularly drunken kid who had passed out was driven away in one of those little golf cart things like an injured football player being taken off the field. He gave the crowd a thumbs up as he was taken away, and we gave him a standing ovation.

ONE YEAR at Slope Day, I was roaming the streets of Ithaca with a few friends when we encountered a severely wasted British dude wandering around in a bathrobe. I asked him if he was OK, and he responded, "If you can stop the world from spinning, I'll pay you." See, even the British know how to party!

LET ME JUST be honest. I have no idea what an imperfect monopoly is, I can't conjugate a Spanish verb, and I can barely spell "calculus," let alone derive anything. But I can buy a keg, tap a keg, fix a keg, pump a keg, and do a kegstand, all with my eyes closed. Ah, the wonders of a college education.

OF COURSE, an essential part of any college experience is the good old-fashioned keg party. The way I look at it, keg parties aren't just fun, they're a sport. First, you have to get to the crowded keg. I use an age-old trick and yell out, "Hey, I live here." That usually gets people out of the way until you run into someone who actually lives there. Then, I usually try some variation of the old "fork-in-the-drawer" trick. Basically, you cut the line but tell people something like, "I need to get a fork from the drawer behind the keg, I swear" so they won't get mad at you. Once you get to the keg, though, you need a cup, and as always, there aren't any. So you just grab a dirty cup that's floating in the keg tub and then offer to fill up the nearest girl's cup for her. As you're filling up, and between all the pushing and people yelling "I live here!" suavely switch the cups. *Voilà*, a perfectly good cup of keg beer. Now, how to get out of the crowd and back to the party . . .

THE ONE THING I hate about parties in college is smelling like smoke all the time. Doesn't it seem like every single person in college smokes cigarettes? It's like they were thinking, OK, well, I don't get enough sleep, I don't eat right, I've never exercised—well, might as well pick up another life-shortening habit while I'm at it! I personally don't smoke, but, inevitably, I come home from a party and as soon as I pull my shirt over my head, there's that nasty smoke smell. Even my shoes smell like smoke. I think I may just take up smoking. It'll be easier that way.

DOES THIS HAPPEN to you? You're at a party, hanging out, drinking a few beers. You sit down, put your half-full cup of beer on the table, and turn to talk to someone. You look back a split second later and notice that there are fifty identical cups of beer on the table and you have no idea which one is yours! Then you start to pick each one up, because you think you know how heavy yours was, but they all feel the same and you can't find yours. Next thing you know you're on your way back to the keg yelling, "Hey, I live here!"

IN A PERSON'S life there are only four times when he or she can experience a week of zero responsibility and extreme drunkenness. This ritual is called Spring Break and it happens once a year in college. Fortunately, I was able to experience this ritual in both Cancún and Acapulco. Mexico is a magical place where the taxis have no meters, the natives don't understand English only when it involves giving you the correct change, and being told what you did last night because you can't remember is more fun than the night itself.

IF YOU WERE going to define the term "scene," you could just show a picture of the pool at our hotel in Acapulco my senior year. It's pretty scary when you get kids from Penn, Wisconsin, Indiana, Arizona, and Syracuse together in one place. I felt like I was back home in Long Island, except everyone was eating nachos and guacamole instead of bagels. The best was watching chicks catfight over the chairs at the pool. I guess they couldn't see that there were 250 other chairs because they were all wearing those stupid purple-tinted sunglasses all the time.

DRUNK KIDS SAY the darndest things. One Spring Break in Cancún, my buddy was absolutely bombed when he met this girl in a club and somehow managed to convince her to leave with him. During the night she kept asking him if he was really drunk, but he denied it. After they hooked up, my friend says to the girl, "Come on, baby, I'll walk you back to your hotel." To which the girl replied, "You idiot, we're in my room!" I love Spring Break.

BACK TO AMERICA—the funny thing about the cops on campus is that they won't allow you to carry open containers of alcohol around campus, unless of course, it's in a brown paper bag. Who came up with this ridiculous law? You can be totally wasted, stumbling into oncoming traffic, with two fake IDs falling out of your pockets, and the cop will be like, "Excuse me, sir, could you come here for a second? Oh, wait, I see you have that bottle of vodka covered up. OK, you're free to go." He's like, "Just a routine paper bag check." Ridiculous.

EVERY ONCE IN A WHILE a college kid will get lucky and a night of irresponsible binge drinking will turn out OK. One night one of my buddies went out and got raging drunk. He woke up the next morning, naked, in a hospital with an IV in his arm. He has no idea how he got there, but the nurse told him, "Well, you put up quite a struggle at first, but then we got you to calm down." When he finally got back from the hospital, he was really upset because he knew that once his parents got the bill and found out what happened, they would kill him. A couple of hours later I'm talking to him and I notice that the hospital bracelet on his arm has someone else's name on it. At some point in the night the nurse must have asked him for ID and my buddy accidentally gave her his fake! So his hospital tag had someone else's name and birth date on it and the bill went to some fake address in New Jersey—and his parents will never even know!

IN THIS NEW century I think there is going to be a greater effort by colleges to cut down on the amount of drinking done by their students. I also think these attempts will fail miserably. This is because administrators think that kids drink because there is nothing else to do. So they try to come up with more sober social options for students, like bowling alleys and museums. The problem is, kids don't drink because there's nothing else to do; they drink because they like getting bombed! If anything, we need more *drinking* options. If schools want to cut down on their students' consumption of alcohol, they should try coming up with something else that makes you forget all your worries and makes ugly chicks look good!

HAVE YOU EVER woken up after a night of partying not knowing whether it is A.M. or P.M.?

PERHAPS THE ONLY thing that limits students' drinking is the almighty hangover. Every college student will experience, at least once, the effects of a killer "morning after." For those that haven't, here are some of the common symptoms: The victim insisting, "I'm never drinking again!" This is of course a blatant lie. Then there is the repeated vomiting, sometimes consisting of things the victim didn't even eat. This mystery has yet to be solved. After a few hours of these symptoms the victim might even become religious, asking if there is a higher power, and if so, why did He create alcohol? Don't worry, this is normal. The best medicine for a hangover is, of course, more drinking. This is known as "drinking through it" or "boot and rally" and works like a charm.

HERE IS a prime example of why alcohol education won't work. I once overheard two girls at a party talking about how one of them repeatedly gets absolutely trashed. One girl said, "Your problem is that you just don't know your limits." To which the other responded, "I know my limits, I just choose to ignore them." I think that eloquently sums up the college experience.

WHY DOESN'T THAT mark you get on your hand when you walk in the bar ever come off? Is it a special pen or something? You have to shower like six times, otherwise everyone knows where you were on Saturday night.

WHEN YOU'RE a guy and you go out to a bar with some of your girlfriends, you automatically become enlisted in the "Rescue Squad." As a member of the Rescue Squad, I was responsible for helping my friends when they were being hit on by guys they didn't like. It works like this: A guy comes over and starts grinding with my friend. She gives me this little eye roll, which is the international signal for "Come rescue me from this disgusting guy," at which point I had to swoop in and pretend to be the girl's boyfriend, brother, or cousin and make the guy leave. The worst, though, is when you're a victim of the Rescue Squad. You'll be hitting on a girl, and some dude will come over and be like, "Yo, man, that's my girlfriend you're dancing with." And you'll be like, "No it's not, dude. Listen, I can tell a rescue when I see one."

THE THING WITH college kids is that although we love to get drunk, we don't necessarily like the physical act of drinking. We need to have some type of game to go along with it. However, there isn't always a Beer Pong table around, so sometimes we have to get creative. Every once in a while one of my buddies would run into my room yelling, "Karo, I need a pair of dice, the ace of spades, and a spatula. We gotta come up with a drinking game fast!"

YOU KNOW WHAT a great moment in college life is? Those two seconds. The two seconds when you first wake up at 3 P.M. after a hard night of partying. Because in those first two seconds you haven't yet remembered that last night you threw up on your floor, punched a cop, and hooked up with an ugly chick. Savor those two seconds as best you can because you can never get them back!

I THINK THAT every college campus has "that bar." You know, that bar that everyone goes to all the time yet everyone complains it sucks and asks why everyone keeps going there? I think we should all stop complaining about "that bar." Embrace it for what it is and accept that you will always go there anyway. And admit it, sometimes it's even fun.

I LOVE "MALE tension" at parties. Guys don't like to meet other guys. Guys think they have all the guy friends they'll ever need and everyone else automatically sucks. You'll see a guy whisper to a girl at a party, "Hey, who's that dude in the corner?" And the girl will say, "Oh, you don't know Matt? He's great." And the guy is always like, "I hate that kid," without ever meeting him!

WHILE GROPING FOR some Tylenol in a hungover state one morning, I had this thought: Why would anyone not buy extra-strength medicine? You roll into the drugstore and they have regular Tylenol and Tylenol Extra

Strength. Obviously, you buy the extra strength. I mean, can you ever have too much strength?

IN THE END, there is nothing better than a night of old-fashioned boozing with your best friends. Going out drinking with my buddies is like being in the cartoon *Snow White and the Seven Drunk Dwarfs*. There's Sloppy, the kid that always pukes at some point in the night; there's Forgetful, the guy who wakes up in a ditch somewhere and can never remember how he got there; there's Angry, the one who gets drunk and tries to fight everyone, no matter how much bigger they are than him; there's Tipsy, the kid who's wasted off two beers; there's Helpful, the kid who never really gets that drunk, so he's always able to help the other dwarfs when they get into trouble; there's Sneezy, the guy who's on antibiotics but drinks anyway and ends up getting twice as hammered as everyone else but can't figure out why; and of course, there's Horny, who has poor judgment when he drinks and thinks he's going home with Snow White but ends up waking up next to a fat chick.

CHAPTER NINE

Studying Here and Abroad

Studying is a very difficult habit for a college student to develop. Anyone can sit in class and take notes. It's studying for exams and writing papers that's the hard part. In fact, the vast majority of time spent in study lounges or libraries consists mainly of looking for papers on the Internet, copying homework assignments, and emailing professors with phony excuses about why you bombed miserably on the last test. I know some kids who spend more time trying to get out of assignments than it would take them to do the actual work!

But junior year, just when you think you can't handle the Friday morning classes, insane professors, and clueless teaching assistants anymore, you get a vacation called Study Abroad. The irony about Study Abroad is that there really isn't much studying involved. It's like your school says, "OK, here are some round-trip tickets to Europe, three A's and an A–, and six months off. Enjoy!" About the only thing that you learn while studying abroad is how to say "Two beers, please" in three different languages.

By the time you get back to the States and senior year rolls around, you've mastered the art of studying.

You know all the best web sites for papers and your professors actually start buying your excuses. For whether studying here or abroad, remember, it's not what you learn, or even the grade you earn, it's the grade you argue for that counts in the end.

HOW FUNNY ARE class readings? At the beginning of the semester you're like, "I'm going to do all the reading for all of my classes and I mean it this time!" About two weeks in, you're like, "OK, I'm going to skim all the readings for half of my classes." By the end of the semester you've lost all your notes and you're using the textbook to even out your coffee table.

WHY IS IT so hard to raise your GPA? I think they make it so it's mathematically impossible to raise it after freshman year. Ever sit down and try to figure out what you need to get in order to raise your GPA to a certain number? It always comes out like you need a 4.6 every semester until you graduate.

THERE IS PROBABLY only one surefire way to improve your grades in college. How? Make an excuse!

I've heard some whoppers in my day, but here's one of my favorites. My buddy did no work for his history class and got a D. So he told the head of the department that he had swollen testicles the whole semester, was in a lot of pain, and was too embarrassed to tell the teacher. He got the grade dropped! I love college.

ISN'T TAKING CLASSES pass/fail great? They should just call it, "Doing as poorly as possible without actually failing," because that's what everyone tries to do anyway! Pass/fail is strange because your reaction to grades is reversed. You get an A and you're like, "Damn, I spent way too much time studying for this." You get a D– and you're like, "Yes! I aced it!"

WHY DO PEOPLE feel the need to take their shoes off while taking a test or studying?

HOW DO PEOPLE miss the last few questions on a test? After an exam, when everyone is talking about what they thought about the test, there's always that one kid who realizes that he missed the last five questions because he didn't look at the last page. How dumb are you?

WHY DON'T I have any classes that have movies as assignments? I have this friend who is a film major. He never studies, never does work, because all he has to do is watch movies. What kind of classes are these? Hey, how about you give me an A for sitting on my ass and doing nothing all day? I see my friend in his room watching TV, relaxing, and drinking a beer and I'm like, "What are you up to?" And he says, "Oh, not much, just doing some homework."

IT SUCKS WHEN you try to argue a final-exam grade that you received in the spring semester when you come back to school after the summer. You walk into the professor's office, he doesn't even remember who you are, you have no idea why you deserve more points because the class was so long ago, and you end up having to make up some excuse about swollen testicles.

MY FRIEND CHANGED majors because the building where all his classes met was too far away. So he switched to a major in a closer building. It's good to know that some of us are making the most of our education.

ANOTHER ONE of my friends tried to be a little too creative. He had an assignment for an English class to write a paper about pretty much anything he wanted. The night before it was due, he went out, got drunk, then came home and wrote a paper about going out, getting drunk, and writing a paper. I think he got a D.

EVER NOTICE THAT the amount of reading you actually do for a class is inversely proportional to the amount that is assigned? Think about it. You sit down to do some reading and you see only six pages or so are assigned, so you read all of it. But if you see that you have fifty pages to read, you're like, "Forget this, I'm not reading any of this crap!"

HOW ARE YOU supposed to register for classes when the course catalogue uses such crazy abbreviations? The classes are listed as like, "Anc. Dem. Hist. Iden. Sem." How am I supposed to know what that is? Similarly, does anyone know how they come up with course numbers? Like, why isn't Sociology 237 called Sociology 238? Who decides that?

THIS IS SOMETHING I have always wondered about. Why does Microsoft Word have all those fonts that are nothing but gibberish? You know, you'll be playing around with the fonts, trying to make a fancy cover page instead of actually writing your paper, and you'll get that Wingdings font that isn't letters, just weird symbols. What the hell is the point of that?

FOR THE MOST part, colleges across America teach western values, such as democracy and equality. So why do all forms of capitalism cease to exist the moment you step into the campus bookstore to sell back your textbooks? How can they give me $10 back for a $100 textbook? What happened to the free-market economy and the laws of supply and demand that we learned so much about? I swear I didn't even want the book, I never even opened it, it's brand-new! And I love when they offer you a really insulting amount of money back, like 75 cents. At first you're like, "Seventy-five cents? No way man, that's ridiculous, I'm just gonna keep the book!" Then you look at this huge textbook that you never used in the first place and you say, "Um, could I get that in quarters?"

IN A LOT of my classes we had a listserv so that the professor could send mass emails to everyone in the class. Inevitably, there's that kid who hits "reply to all" and sends a message to the whole class that was meant only for the professor. And it's always something really embarrassing like, "Dear Professor Carpenter: Unfortunately, this semester I was stricken with a case of swollen testicles . . ."

STUDYING ABROAD IS another essential part of the college experience. The summer after my sophomore year I studied abroad in London. The hardest part about arranging the trip was calling over there with the time difference. I had to call between like 4 A.M. and 11 A.M. Those are the worst times for a college student. At 11 A.M. I'm sleeping and at 4 A.M. I'm either drunk or sleeping, so it was kind of difficult. I ended up just emailing instead.

I KNOW A PLACE where there is no sexism or racism. Where people are not judged by their appearance or religion or anything. It is the world of finding subletters for your apartment to live there when you go abroad. I was looking for anyone with a pulse and a wallet to live in my room while I was gone. I think if everyone was looking for subletters the world would be a better place.

COLLEGE LIFE in England is a lot different than here in the States. First of all, the drinking age is eighteen and there was a bar in the dorm that I was staying in. A bar in the dorm! A dream come true! The British are obviously more responsible drinkers than we are, because if there were bars in every dorm in America and the legal age were eighteen, we'd be the drunkest humans on earth! No one would do work, no one would graduate. Everyone would be wasted all the time. It would be great.

I HAD TO FLY home from London for a weekend because I had to go to a wedding. I actually brought my laundry all the way home with me on the plane. What can I say? I just don't know how to do laundry!

THE BRITISH HAVE some very interesting slang. They don't get wasted, they get "pissed." Kids kept telling me how pissed they were—I'm pissed, she's pissed, he's pissed. I always thought everyone was mad at me. Turns out they were just drunk.

WHEN TRAVELING during your Study Abroad program, there's always that kid who thinks he can force others to speak English. When I was in Paris, my friend Jason would go to the ticket window and say, "Two round-trip tickets please." The dude would say something in French that we couldn't understand, so my friend would scream back, "*Two-round trip tickets!*" Like yelling is going to make him understand English.

EVEN I WAS not immune to the occasional dumb-ass comment while overseas. While in London, I was talking to some British kids about drinking games. I asked them, "So, do you guys play quarters?" And this guy said, "We don't even have quarters here." What a stupid American I am.

AT PENN MOST kids go abroad the first semester of their junior year and not over the summer like me, so by second semester they've all come back and those of us who stayed behind have to hear all their stories. After a while you don't even have to listen anymore, you can just fill in the blanks: "Yeah, man, I just got back from [insert European city here] and it was so [insert foreign slang meaning "great" that the person is using to show off]! The beer there is so [insert "cheap" or "expensive"] and we got so wasted! And I hooked up with [insert blatantly untrue amount] girls there! I met up with [insert name of other friend who already told you this story] in [insert Amsterdam/Oktoberfest/Prague] and we got bombed all weekend." I'm like, thanks for the info, dude, but I've heard this one already.

YOU CAN ALWAYS tell which people went abroad and where they went because they feel the need to plaster their room with flags, posters, pictures, and other crap from where they were. Yeah, that's great buddy, but you're back in the United States now and we don't really care.

ONE PROBLEM I have is that, for some people, I have no idea if they were abroad or not. I'll be like, "So, Dina, how was Australia?" And she'll say, "Karo, I had class with you last semester." Oops.

ANYWAY, BACK TO AMERICA. I always get a kick out of kids in the honors program at school. First of all, how the hell can colleges have an honors program in the first place? Are these kids getting the "real" knowledge? It's like you walk into office hours and mention the honors program, and the professor says, "Oh, why didn't you mention you were an honors student earlier? Let me give you this special textbook and teach you what's really going on. Everything in the non–honors class I teach is made up." Am I the only one who realizes this whole honors thing is a conspiracy? Some honors classes even have a special curve, it's something absurd like 75 percent A's, 25 percent B's, and nothing below that. Therefore, all the honors kids have inflated GPAs because their curve is so easy. So now the school can go, "Hey, look at our honors kids, their GPAs are so much higher than the regular kids, you see, we knew they were special."

FOR THE MOST PART, college kids are a pretty intellectual bunch. There are engineering students learning about the latest technologies. There are biology majors learning every minute detail about the human body. And there are business students studying the most complicated finance problems. There is one thing we all have in common, though. We have no clue what the hell is going on in the world. During your time in college, current events suddenly become your last priority. Revolutions are occurring, wars are being fought, history-making decisions are being made, and we're living in a happy little bubble where the worst news of the day is that liquor prices went up at the store down the block.

I DON'T THINK people realize when they're being annoying in the study lounge. Kids are eating the loudest foods, like cracking open peanuts and chowing down on huge bags of Doritos. And then they whisper. The damn whispering. Do you not understand that in a specially designated, dead-quiet room in the corner of campus, in the basement of a building, in the middle of the night during finals week that if you whisper, everyone can hear you? So, I try to give the little polite hints. The sigh. The stare. The sigh combined with the stare. But they don't get it—they just stare back at you with that stupid grin that says, "What, do I have Doritos in my teeth?"

I ONCE GOT a D+ on a paper. I just don't get that. I mean, the paper sucked, don't get me wrong, but how does a professor come up with a D+? What's with the plus? A B+, that I understand. That means, "You did pretty good but not good enough to get an A." D– is OK too. That means, "You suck really badly, but not badly enough to fail." But a D+, what the hell is that? The professor is basically saying, "I'm not quite sure what to make of this paper, but I definitely know it sucked to some extent." Whatever, I was taking the class pass/fail anyway!

I ALWAYS HEAR these stories about crazy stuff happening in the library: guys getting head in the computer lab from random girls, kids getting laid in the study lounge in the middle of the day. Who are these people? Why does this never happen to me? Maybe I'm studying in the wrong place.

GROUP PROJECTS in high school were harmless. You went to the house of some kid in your class who lived down the block from you. You felt pretty safe. Maybe his mom even made you cookies. But in college, group projects are a little scary. I go to a big school, I don't know who these kids are. I'm going to some strange dude's house in the middle of Philadelphia, no one knows where I'm going, this kid could be a psycho or something. Hey, maybe he'll have cookies.

AS IF GETTING your grades back at the end of the semester isn't bad enough, at Penn we have an automated telephone system. So you call up and put in your information and it tells you, in the slowest and most suspenseful way possible, how badly you screwed up the semester. It'll be like, "Your grade for Eco-no-mics . . . one-zero-one . . . section one-twenty-two . . . is . . . ["Please give me a B, please!"] . . . C . . . ["Damn! C'mon, give me the C+, gimme the plus!"] . . . minus . . . repeat . . . C minus . . . C minus . . ." And you think to yourself, Next time I'll just wait for my grades in the mail.

I AM ALWAYS amazed by the fact that people go home right after their last final exam. It absolutely blows my mind. Why the hell would you want to go right home after you've been studying for two weeks straight? What is there to do at home? Nothing! I always stay a minimum of two days after my last final and just get bombed. That way I make sure that I don't retain any of the information I learned during the semester.

CHAPTER TEN

The Life and Times

I've made road trips to many colleges around the country. I've also interacted with tons of college students around the world because of my web site. The fact is, the life and times of college students everywhere are remarkably similar. For the most part, all we really want to do is hook up fairly regularly and maybe, if we're lucky, get our damn computers to work properly.

By day, we're online, instant-messaging our friends, downloading music and porn, fending off the computer viruses that come with the music and porn, and accidentally sending sexually explicit emails intended for our frat brothers to our parents. After all, the Internet has not only provided college students with an incredible resource, but also another way to waste time and avoid doing any work.

By night our one and only goal is to hook up randomly. Seven nights a week are spent trying to get someone into your extra-long twin bed. Where we go is solely determined by which members of the opposite sex will be there. Everything we say and do revolves around the possibility of hooking up. We drink heavily and encourage others to do the same, hoping that with everyone's inhibitions and common sense drowned in a pool of alcohol, maybe we'll get lucky and not have to rely on all the porn we downloaded during the day.

ISN'T IT TERRIBLE that you are always bragging to your friends at other colleges how awesome your school is, and then when they finally come to visit, it's the worst weekend ever? And you try to explain to them that it's not usually like this, but they totally don't believe you.

IS IT A GENERAL RULE that after you become a junior in college you always tuck your shirt into your pants? Just look around: freshmen and sophomores are untucked, juniors and seniors are tucked. And it gets worse too. Your dad's pants are above his belly button and your grandfather's pants are up to his nipples.

Eventually, you don't even have to wear a shirt anymore!

THERE ARE MANY universal rules that college kids across the nation live by. Here are two: No matter what else is on TV, a college guy will always stop and watch either *SportsCenter* or *The Simpsons*. A universal rule for girls? At some point during college every girl will cut their hair really short . . . and then proceed to complain about it for the next two months like they didn't know what it was going to look like.

MY NAME IS Aaron Karo. My email address at school was:

aaronkar@wharton.upenn.edu

They couldn't give me the last letter of my name? Now I have the dumbest address ever. Who the hell comes up with these things anyway? I want my *o!*

THE THING WITH EMAIL is that it's so easy to screw up so hugely. Case in point: One time I wrote this fairly long letter to one of my good friends, describing in detail my partying and what the girls call me after a night in bed. And then I accidentally sent it to my English professor! The worst part is that when the accidental receiver writes back, it's always something embarrassing like, "Nice message, Big Daddy."

WHO ARE THESE people who punctuate every sentence in an email with a :) or :o ? What the hell is that? If you're happy or excited, just write it out instead of making me decipher a goddamn semicolon face. What are you, a mime?

AND WHAT IS this crap that some people have following all their emails? You know, it's got their name and phone number and email address and school address and home address and instant messenger screen name and ICQ number and Dave Matthews song lyrics and pictures of their dog made with commas and exclamation points. Thanks, but I don't need your life story every time you send me an email.

HAVE YOU EVER been sitting in the library, sending an email to your friend, and you realize as you read the email before you send it that it reads like a second-grader wrote it? There's no punctuation, whole words are missing, and nothing is spelled right. It's like when you send emails, you become temporarily illiterate.

FOR SOME REASON my friends find it funny to email me all these porn videos. For instance, I once got one of a girl having sex with a horse. Now that was just what I needed before lunch! I've been sent so many pornos that I think my computer has a virus. No, not like a computer virus, an actual sexually transmitted disease. Right now I'm wearing a full body condom just to type this.

I LOVE IT when I'm in a friend's room and he calls me over to look at something he found on the Internet— and then proceeds to read it out loud while I'm looking right over his shoulder. I'm right next to you—I can read it myself!

WHY DO PEOPLE insist on sending me the dumbest email forwards? Just when I think that I've seen them all, one of my friends sends another one. Sometimes it's a good-luck tiger or a magical turtle. Other times it's one of the biggest hoaxes ever, like Bill Gates is giving away money or some dude in Texas needs a liver. And people actually believe they're true! My friend comes running into my room saying that he got a chain letter and if he doesn't send it on to ten people, something terrible will happen. I'm like, "Sorry, dude, but something terrible has already happened to you—you're a gullible idiot!"

THIS KID in one of my classes was telling me that the previous semester he had a pretty serious girlfriend. One day this guy is just fooling around on the Internet and searches for his girlfriend's name. Turns out she has a personal homepage. What's on it? Pictures of her other boyfriend from home! Oops.

ONE DAY I was talking to a friend of mine who is a grad student at Penn. I asked him if there were any hot girls in his classes, where most of the students are like twenty-seven or twenty-eight years old. He told me that there is this one really cute girl, but she's married. Married? I can't even fathom that kind of commitment at this point! I asked him if there was any chance he could hook me up with her. He didn't seem to think so.

WHY CAN GIRLS never be trusted to tell you if their friend is cute or not? They never give you a straight answer. It's always something like, "Oh, she's really sweet" or "Well, she has a pretty face." Translated into guy's terms, these phrases usually mean "This chick is busted."

I'VE NOTICED ONE distinct difference between guys and girls when it comes to hooking up. If a guy and girl come home together, the girl expects the room to be empty and won't do anything if there are people around. Guys, on the other hand, could care less. Their roommates could be in the room playing poker and taking pictures and the guy will just be like, "Oh don't worry, my roommates are asleep."

WHY DO MY FRIENDS call me late at night and then ask if they're interrupting me and a girl? First of all, if I was hooking up, do you think I'd pick up the phone? Second of all, if you thought I was hooking up, why did you call me in the first place?

THE WONDERFUL and at the same time excruciating period of time during college when I had a girlfriend made me realize that everything I do—get dressed, bathe, go to class, go out—I do to meet girls. When I have a girl, I don't want to bother with those things. I just sit around unshaven in my underwear all day and don't leave the house. Hmm, now that I think of it, I haven't heard from my girlfriend in a while. Uh-oh.

I THINK I have figured college relationships out. As you get more serious with someone, you start sleeping over at their place a lot. Which is great, but you're always hooking up, so you don't really wash up before bed. And you come home together after a night of partying and go right to bed. Personal hygiene takes a back seat to the relationship. Pretty soon you both start to smell. That's when you have to decide if you are going to start leaving a toothbrush at the other person's place. And that's a big decision, because if you do, that means you are really getting serious. But if you don't bring the toothbrush, pretty soon you can't stand the other person's smell and you break up. The Toothbrush Phase is an important turning point in any relationship.

THE THING ABOUT college is that college kids don't really date so much as we randomly hook up. The worst is when you want to stop hooking up with someone because it's like you have to break up when you weren't even going out in the first place. You're like, "Listen, I don't think this is working out. We get along really well, but we're seeing each other all the time. I'm starting to get too much out of this relationship."

MY BIGGEST PET PEEVE of all time is when my friends leave long and detailed instructions on their answering-machine messages like, "Hi, you've reached Marcia at 555-3958. I'm either on the other line or I can't get to the phone right now, but please leave your name, number, time that you called, along with a detailed message after the tone, and I will call you back as soon as I can." Thanks for the instructions, but do you think I've never used one of these things before?

WHY DO KIDS freak out when they realize that they're wearing the same shirt as someone else? I go over to my friend's room to pre-game wearing a red shirt, and (oh no!) my friend is wearing a red shirt too! Here we go: "You can't wear the same shirt as me! I'm not going out like this! I was wearing the red shirt first, you have to change!" Take it easy, dude, we just won't stand next to each other.

I THINK IT'S funny when kids who go to schools that use a trimester system try to say it's not that bad. So let's figure this out. At the end of the summer you're home alone for a whole month while everyone else is back partying at school. And by the time the last trimester is over, everyone else has already been enjoying summer for a month. Plus you have a midterm or a final about every other week. The kids are always defending it, saying, "Oh, well, um, it's cool, because you get to take fewer classes at a time." Yeah, right. Sorry, buddy, trimesters suck!

I KIND OF FEEL BAD for people who go to colleges that no one has ever heard of. I sort of have that problem because when I say I go to Penn, people are always like, "Penn State? Good football team, huh?" And I'm like, "No, the University of Pennsylvania, you idiot." We actually have shirts at the bookstore that have the Penn logo, and on top it says NOT PENN STATE. Anyway, whenever I ask someone where they go and they say some random college like, oh, South Rockford

University, I never know what to say. I'm always like, "Oh . . . good old South Rockford. Good football team, huh?"

CHAPTER ELEVEN

Senior

Year

Remember the second half of your senior year in high school? You didn't do much work, you probably cut a bunch of classes, you may have even gotten wasted in the middle of the day. You had "senioritis." Well, the college version of senioritis is much crazier (or should I say, lazier). My friends didn't do anything. Some weren't even enrolled in classes. I once went a whole week without leaving my apartment. Being a second-semester senior is truly the life. Graduation is still a few months away, you don't have a care in the world, and you're still getting money from your parents. What could be better?

I had virtually graduated by my last semester, so the two classes I took were pretty much for show. Both met only on Mondays, both were pass/fail, one was geography and the other was taught by my frat brother's dad. I did nothing and life was good. It's funny because when you're in the midst of senioritis, you can't comprehend why anyone else is doing work or studying. You'll walk by the library on your way to Happy Hour and think, What are all those people doing in there? Are they doing work? I don't understand—I'm not doing anything, why are they?

My last few months of college were great. But when I look back upon my senioritis-infested final semester, I do wish I had taken advantage of my time a little better. I probably shouldn't have taken geography.

AS I BEGAN my senior year, I couldn't help but laugh at the freshmen, how they travel in herds and drink until they land in the hospital. But as I was going to a party with about seven or eight friends, most of whom consistently drink until unconscious, I thought, Damn, not much has changed!

AT THE END of my sophomore year I moved out of the frat house, which was near the center of campus, and into an off-campus apartment where I lived until graduation. At Penn the off-campus apartments are about five blocks from the center of campus. If you think about it, it doesn't really make much sense to live off-campus—it takes longer to get to class and the houses are a lot crappier. It's like, congratulations, you're an upperclassman, now you get to walk farther and live dirtier. Thanks a lot.

WHEN I LIVED off-campus, I lived with nine other guys in a four-story house and no one would get the door. Ever. The kids on the fourth floor claimed they were too far away. The kids on the second floor complained that they always had to get the door and then refused to do it. And the kids on the third floor were just plain lazy. We hated getting the door so much that if anyone ever came over more than once we just made them a key.

MY HOUSE ALSO had a bit of a mouse problem. Seems that some of my housemates thought that leaving food and trash on the floor was OK. (Some of this may have stemmed from the fact that we carried our fridge up two flights of stairs and put it in the hallway so that no one would have to go very far to get to it—hey, we're lazy.) Anyway, our rodents had so much to feed on that they evolved into a species of supermice. Not only did they flip over traps and steal whole sandwiches; when we went to sleep at night, they went to mouse school and had mouse parties. There were police mice and teacher mice and even mice that drove around in little mouse cars. I think they were plotting to take over the house. Now if only we could have taught them to get the door . . .

YOU KNOW WHAT one of the best parts of senior year is? Hooking up with your friends. It's like, OK, we made it this far, we've had a great time, we've laughed together, we've cried together, now let's just get naked. Because that's one of the essential goals of college, right? Trying to see as many people naked as possible. Come the end of senior year, you look around the bar, and you're like, I've seen most of these people naked before. So you turn to your friend next to you and say, "So, what are you up to later?"

DO YOU REMEMBER when you bought your computer freshman year? It was so powerful, and if you were in a dorm with a high-speed Internet connection, you could download porn in like two seconds. What the hell happened? Almost three and a half years later, my computer sucks. Connecting to the Internet is like a slow death, all those pornos gave my computer a sexually transmitted disease and I've spilled at least a six-pack worth of beer on the keys. By my senior year I just used the thing as a coaster.

I LOVE COLLEGE traditions. At Penn my favorite tradition is definitely Hey Day. Hey Day occurs on the last day of classes and is when the juniors symbolically become seniors. The entire junior class, wearing bright red shirts, Styrofoam hats, and armed with wooden canes, gets up at 9 A.M., drinks heavily, and marches around campus beating each other with the canes and breaking everything. At the end of the day the juniors are declared seniors. Sounds strange, but what I can remember of it made it my favorite day in all four years of college. My friend got cut with a cane, so I took him to the hospital. The doctor said that it was the twelfth cane-related injury so far that day. At that moment I was so proud to be a senior.

I THINK SENIORITIS was accurately summed up by my friend David. When he was a senior and I was a sophomore, I saw him in the frat house cramming for the last real exam he would ever have to take. He remarked to me, "Karo, if I get through this test, I'm never trying again." I always tried to follow his example when I became a senior.

MY SENIOR YEAR I was pretty much addicted to drinking Red Bull and vodka. I had never been much of a fan of vodka. But then along comes Red Bull, this magical drink that covers the taste completely and is available for free at my school (if you buy it at the commissary and charge it to your ID card). I was also obsessed with that TV show *Temptation Island,* which has to be one of the greatest shows ever! So I guess that's what my senior year was reduced to: downing vodka–caffeine-drink cocktails while watching reality television on FOX. Man, that's pretty embarrassing.

MIDWAY THROUGH SENIOR YEAR I started to feel really old. But not because I was about to graduate and enter the real world or because the freshmen looked so young. It was because I found out that half of my friends were on Propecia. What the hell is going on here? When did everyone's hair start falling out? I walk into a party and it feels like the Hair Club for Men.

TOWARD THE END of my last semester of college, I was deep in the throes of senioritis. I needed to go to the library to take out a book, but I hadn't been there in almost two years. So I'm wandering around aimlessly and this librarian spots me and asks if everything is all right. I'm like, "Well, I have no idea where I am or what I'm doing." So she says, "Oh, are you a freshman?" And I tell her, "No, ma'am, I'm a graduating senior." She looks at me like she has seen this a thousand times before and says, "Well, that explains a lot. First things first, you're in the women's bathroom . . ."

SENIOR YEAR, A lot of my friends started looking at graduate schools and taking entrance exams. Some were more excited than others. When my buddy Jay got a package in the mail, he was psyched because he thought it was a new video game. When he saw that it was his tremendous LSAT study guide instead, he commented, "I'd rather this was a mail bomb."

I LOVE HOW law school becomes the default for college seniors who have no idea what they want to do after graduation. I'll be like, "So, Zach, what are you doing with your life?" And he'll say, "Oh, I don't know what the hell I want to do, so I'm just applying to law school." Some kids don't even go that far. They're just taking the LSATs. I'll be like, "So, Ingrid, I hear you're going to law school?" And she'll reply, "Well, not exactly, but I am taking the LSATs. Well, I'm thinking about taking the LSATs. OK, I haven't thought about it all, but that's what I told my mom."

I'VE PREVIOUSLY MENTIONED "that bar." You know, that bar on campus that everyone goes to all the time? Everyone complains that it sucks, but keeps going back there anyway. "That bar" at Penn is called Smokey Joe's. Smokes has been around forever and we really did go there all the time. With a couple of weeks to go until graduation, I was at Smokes and noticed that there was a digital countdown clock on the wall. At first I just thought it was counting down to the next St. Patrick's Day or something and didn't pay much attention. Then a bunch of us realized it was counting down to graduation—our graduation. This was unacceptable of course, and my friend ended the travesty by smashing the clock with a beer bottle. In fact, every time I'm in Smokes I make it a point to stop the clock. Being in "that bar" every night is bad enough without being reminded of how little time we have left!

SO IT'S BEEN over three years of college and I still can't remember anyone's name, to the point where I don't even bother listening anymore. Cell phones now present an additional problem, though, because when I get a girl's number in a bar, I put it in my phone. When I get to the part where you input the name, I just put in *X* and hope she doesn't notice.

I'M ALSO IN an interesting situation because the memory on my cell phone is full. So every time I want to put a new number in, I have to delete one that's already in there. So when I meet someone at a bar, I have to basically scroll through all the people I know, pick the one I like least, and delete them. It's kind of like cell phone *Survivor.*

AS A WISE old senior, I have some scheduling advice for those younger than me. You know that really great class that you've always wanted to take but it's only offered at 9 A.M.? Don't take it, it's not worth it, you'll end up sleeping through the whole class anyway. Similarly, thinking of scheduling all your classes early so that you'll have the whole day free? Guess how you'll spend all that free time: napping. Why do I have such views? Because in college you only go to bed at 4 A.M. or when you're wasted, whichever comes first. I had this friend who needed to get to bed early one night because he had a test the next day, and he couldn't fall asleep until he chugged three beers first.

MY DAD CAN'T WAIT for me to graduate and start working. You see, there's a tradition in the Karo family that when you get your first real job and get your first paycheck, you have to take the whole family out to a really nice dinner. My dad has been holding this dinner over my head since I was like eight years old. I'd be going to Little League practice or something, and my dad would be like, "Oh, you're gonna buy me some steak dinner one day, son, I can't wait!" No pressure or anything, Dad!

UNFORTUNATELY, SENIOR YEAR for many people is filled with endless job interviews. It would be pretty funny if you could go in there and just tell the flat-out truth. It would probably go something like this:

INTERVIEWER: So, Brad, what kind things do you do outside of the classroom?

BRAD: Well, to be honest, I spend most of my time binge drinking and trying to get laid.

INTERVIEWER: Hmm, OK, well what did you like most about this marketing course that you took?

BRAD: Actually, I never went to that class. It was at noon and I don't get up before 2 P.M., you know?

INTERVIEWER: Right. Well, Brad, tell me, why exactly are you interested in working for this company?

BRAD: Well, I'm not really even sure what you guys do, I just really need the money. Hey, how much longer is this going to take? Because it's almost Happy Hour and I've got to go.

SENIORITIS ASIDE, my last day of college was dramatic to say the least. As I mentioned, I only took two classes my last semester, both pass/fail. However, in one of the classes, I got a D on the midterm. Which was fine, except the only other assignment was a presentation at the end of the semester that counted for much of my final grade. Two days prior to the presentation I realized that if I messed it up, I could feasibly fail the presentation, the class, and then not graduate! Considering I had not even started preparing, this was bad, really bad. The presentation was at night, and I had to show up wearing a tuxedo since I had a sorority formal directly afterward. I was sweating profusely. As I stepped to the podium, I saw my college career flash before my eyes. One false move and next thing I knew I'd be in summer school. I wiped my brow, fumbled my shoddily prepared notes in front of me, and began to speak. And then, it happened—the professor fell asleep! I was saved! I stumbled through the presentation for about five minutes, and then when the professor started to come to, I adjusted my bow tie and said, ". . . and that is how I would solve the campaign finance reform problem." He had no idea what happened, so I passed with flying colors! I love college.

I THINK YOU can pretty much classify graduating seniors in three categories. First, those going off to slave away at full-time jobs (also known as "trying to work as much as possible in order to get as rich as possible as fast as possible"). Second, those who are taking a year off to figure out what they want to do with their lives (also known as "let's see how long I can mooch off my parents before they realize I just sit on the couch all day"). And third, those doing a little bit of both (also known as "going to grad school"). By the way, if you don't know which of these categories you fit into, you're probably in the second one.

ONE OF THE BEST PARTS of senior year is Senior Week. Senior Week is the week after finals but before graduation when all the seniors stick around to booze and reminisce about four years of drunken mayhem. The funny thing about Senior Week is that since you're the only ones on campus, you finally get to find out which kids are actually seniors. As it turned out, half of the kids I thought were seniors were only sophomores and all the kids I thought were juniors were really seniors. Of course by the end of Senior Week you're so sloshed you don't care who's who, much less how old they are.

SENIOR WEEK CONSISTED of many school-sponsored events, such as an open-bar formal and a twenty-bar pub crawl. (I made it to bar sixteen until being "removed" from the festivities.) I'm thinking, how can the school pay for, sponsor, and in fact encourage such activities? It's like they spent the last four years trying to figure out anything that would make us drink less and then comes Senior Week they're just like, "OK, we give up, you guys are just alcoholics, we can't stop you. In fact, we feel kinda bad about being such hardasses these past four years, so you know what? Get out there and get bombed. On the house." Weird.

THEN, INEVITABLY, CAME GRADUATION. Perhaps because I had recorded the four-year drunken odyssey of my graduating class on my web site, I was chosen to deliver a commencement address at my graduation ceremony. It was one of the most amazing experiences of my life. Of course, I was so nervous up there I barely remember any of it. I do remember, though, how funny it was during the ceremony when everyone was trying to signal to their parents in the crowd where they were sitting. I'm on my cell phone like, "Hey, Mom, I'm wearing a black cap and a long robe and I'm sitting next to a flag." And my mom would say, "Oh, I see you! We're sitting on the left side of the stadium and your father is wearing a blue hat." And of course, I spotted them right away. I saw the huge smile on my dad's face and tears coming from my mom's eyes, and that's when I knew it was all over. They would never give me money ever again.

AS I LOOK back on my college career, I know that I could not have spent it at a better place than Penn. Not only did I have the time of my life, I got a hell of an education as well. I do have one regret, though. Never being a tour guide. I know that sounds kind of dorky, but the one thing that I always wanted to do was be a tour guide and show wide-eyed high school kids my amazing world. I'd be walking backward through campus, trying to avoid the slow walkers and big-backpack people, and saying, "In that building, that's where I pulled my first all-nighter. And in that dorm over there, that's where I lost my virginity. See that liquor store down the block? I once got negged there three times in one night." And we'd walk past my fraternity house where all my brothers would probably throw beer cans at the tour and past "that bar" Smokey Joe's and around the spot where I once threw up for an hour straight, and

I'd tell these pre-froshes all my ridiculous stories. And the pre-froshes would be like, "Wow, Karo, is this what college life is really like? I can't wait!" And I'd respond, "Kid, you have no idea what you're in for."

Is There Life After College?

The summer after you graduate from college is depressing. You realize that grad school or your new job is just around the corner. And you can no longer wake up to find a keg in your bathroom. It's sad.

Before I moved away from home, though, my parents threw me a big graduation party. It was pretty cool. I had a ton of liquor and a bunch of kegs in my backyard (though none of them ended up in the bathroom). It was at this party that I realized just how bitter college graduates really are. Sure, I got a bunch of handshakes and pats on the back from the adults at the party, but each time they were accompanied by a whisper in the ear like, "Welcome to the real world kid, the party's over!" or "Congratulations, Aaron, but it's all downhill from here!" They wouldn't even let me enjoy my own party! A couple of weeks later, however, reality set in and I moved out for good. Life as I knew it changed forever.

Just about five months after graduation, I was given a second chance. A chance to relive the glory days, if only for a weekend. That chance was called Homecoming. Homecoming is very strange, because it is the first time since you were a pre-frosh that you're at college but don't actually go there. You're tentative because you don't know everyone anymore and things have changed. For example, "that bar." By the time I returned to Penn, "that bar" was practically empty because some cheese steak place down the block was converted into a club. I went in for a sandwich and ended up at Happy Hour. It was weird. Then there are all the fellow alums who run up to you saying, "Hey, Karo, how have you been? We've got to hang out this weekend!" I'd say, "Dude, we never hung out when we went to college, why start now?"

As I wandered through campus and checked out the freshmen dorms (hey, I was doing research for the book!), I realized that things would never go back to the way they were. For instance, college is the only place on earth where the phrases "I'm sorry, I was wasted" or "Hey, I'm in this frat, wanna go upstairs?" actually work. Believe me, I've tried since. More important, though, I realized that the reason college will never be the same after you graduate is that you will never be the same after you graduate. During your time at college your life is like a screwed-up spin cycle: Sleep, Beer, Eat, Work, Beer, repeat as necessary. After graduation, you're hungry, tired, and hungover and you will never quite recover. But what a hell of a ride it was.

You only get four years. Make the most of them. I know I did.

—Karo
June 2002
New York City